# EMPOWERED
## FROM ABOVE

# EMPOWERED
## FROM ABOVE

GEORGE BLOOMER

WHITAKER
HOUSE

All Scripture quotations are taken from the King James Version (KJV) of the Bible.

## EMPOWERED FROM ABOVE

To contact the author for speaking engagements, please write to:
George Bloomer
515 Dowd St.
Durham, NC 27701


ISBN: 0-88368-285-0
Printed in the United States of America
© 2002 by George G. Bloomer


Whitaker House
30 Hunt Valley Circle
New Kensington, PA 15068
web site: www.whitakerhouse.com


Library of Congress Cataloging-in-Publication Data Pending

1 2 3 4 5 6 7 8 9 10 11 / 10 09 08 07 06 05 04 03 02

# Table of Contents

# Introduction

# Introduction

*Greater is he that is in you, than he that is in the world.*
—1 John 4:4

Who is this "greater One" that John was talking about? It is the Spirit of Christ—the Holy Spirit! If you've surrendered your life to Christ, you have received the abundant gifts that His Spirit brings. The fruit of the Spirit—love, joy, peace, longsuffering, kindness, goodness, faithfulness, gentleness, self-control—is growing on the branches of your life. (See Galatians 5:22–23.) You live in an awareness of His presence and trust in the power that He gives.

Jesus Himself relied on the Holy Spirit as His source of power. Acts 10:38 says, *"God anointed Jesus of Nazareth with the Holy Ghost and with power: who went about doing good, and healing all that were oppressed of the devil; for God was with him."* What about you? Are you involved in the Father's business? Are you working for the kingdom of heaven with the same power that Jesus depended upon? Are you walking in His footsteps and carrying out the Great Commission that He left for His followers?

To be a witness for Christ, you must know who you are in Him. Those within the kingdom of darkness must also recognize who you are and where you stand. You need a reputation for having power and protection that comes from dying to self and living under the blood of your Savior. This assurance comes from the Holy Spirit. The repercussions of the power and protection that He gives are vast. As Acts 1:8 teaches, *"But ye shall receive power, after that the Holy Ghost is come upon you: and ye shall be witnesses unto me both in Jerusalem...and unto the uttermost part of the earth."*

It is only through the Holy Spirit that you can walk in the authority that Christ has gifted to you. Even in times of distress, when you don't quite know what to pray for because you're too distraught or too consumed with stressful situations, the Holy Spirit will step in and intercede for you. *"Likewise the Spirit also helpeth our infirmities: for we know not what we should pray for as we ought: but the Spirit itself maketh intercession for us with groanings which cannot be uttered"* (Romans 8:26).

Perhaps you've already begun to experience the fullness of the Holy Spirit. You've received baptism from above and have tasted the Spirit's filling in your life. You too must ask yourself, Am I doing the Father's business? Simply receiving the Spirit does not ensure that you are walking in His ways. As Paul made clear in one of his epistles, having the Spirit's gifts in our lives means nothing if we don't show the Spirit's fruit as well. *"Though I speak with the tongues of men and of angels, and have not charity, I am become as sounding brass, or a tinkling cymbal"* (1 Corinthians 13:1).

Some years ago, not long after I had received the baptism of the Holy Spirit with the gift of speaking in tongues, I was selected by God to be carried in the spirit several times over the course of a month. During this time I received revelation on the heavens in the form of dreams. These dreams, which I later came to recognize as visions, came at the end of a fifty-day consecration fast leading up to the Day of Pentecost. With these dreams, it was as if the heavens opened up to me. God revealed much to me about the Holy Spirit, His nature, and His ways of working. This book records the contents of those dreams, as well as the understanding gleaned from them.

Through the revelation of this book, I pray that we will begin to understand the benefits of baptism in the Holy Spirit, in all its fullness. I pray too that we will not reduce it to an excuse for speaking in tongues, dancing around the church, or being slain in the spirit. Instead, may we recognize that the Holy Spirit is fully God, who comes to live, reign, and rule in us. He, the Spirit of Truth, is a teacher, a leader, an energizer of strength within our souls. May we rightly understand the Holy Spirit in the fullness of His character. May we yield ourselves to His working, as He moves in our lives according to His timing. The time has come to reject myths and to let go of questionable traditions. Allow scriptural knowledge to intervene, and learn what it really means to be baptized from above!

*I pray for you today to be filled with all godliness and true revelation that can be released only through and by the Holy Spirit. I pray the convicting power of the Holy Spirit upon you that will destroy any stronghold that might be lying dormant in your life. Right now we claim this house—your temple—for the glory of God. We sweep it and cleanse it and forbid any demonic forces from returning to this place. Through the power and the anointing of the Holy Ghost, I pray for revelation knowledge to come upon you—the word of wisdom, the word of knowledge, and the word of prophecy—that healing will be your portion and deliverance your lifestyle. In Jesus' name, Amen.*

# The Dream

---

# Seven Days in the Spirit

# The Dream

# Seven Days in the Spirit

## Day One

In my first dream I saw people standing all around the world. I could tell I was seeing the whole world because it was daytime in some areas and nighttime in others. The people wore many types of clothing as well. I recognized people from Turkey, Russia, Mexico, Palestine, Africa, and many other countries.

My dream was filled with music. I saw the heavens, or what appeared to be the heavens. I saw bouquets of color. Colors and colors and colors and colors were shooting out of the heavens. I can only explain what I experienced in terms of color and music. Some colors I can't even describe. I don't have words to tell you about the most beautiful yellows, greens, oranges, reds, and purples. Jasper. Ruby red. Emerald green. Magenta. Just colors, colors, colors. And the sounds were heavenly: trumpets, harps, drums, and violins.

When I passed through heaven's entrance, I saw more colors. The streets were pure, pure as can be. There was no gold pavement on the streets—but there was no crime, either. I heard voices, the many voices of my childhood as if

15

kids were playing outside. As I walked through the streets, I drew nearer to what appeared to be ancient medieval buildings. They were all made of sapphire bricks. I have absolutely no idea what these monuments were. As I passed through the gate of the sapphire bricked walls, though, the voices changed. I heard voices of adults as they instructed their children, passing down their morals and values; voices of people talking business; and voices of thinkers discussing philosophies and ideas. Still, I could see no people.

I continued walking, guided by an inner-conscience, and approached what appeared to be a platform with steps, each step displaying colors of a heavenly rainbow. There were gifts too, wrapped up in the colors of Christmas, Easter, and Valentine's Day. Gifts were everywhere. Tons and tons and tons of them! The packages were of different sizes—some the size of cars, some the size of buildings, some as small as a calculator, and some the size of a shoe box—but all of them were wrapped up. And the voices changed; they said, "Where do we deliver this?" and, "Waiting on a pick-up." It was as if I were at a shipping company, looking at a graveyard of packages that had been misplaced and couldn't be delivered.

As I mounted the platform and left behind the unclaimed gifts, I passed through a door and suddenly began falling. It wasn't falling, though; I realized, instead, that I was being carried swiftly to another level by what appeared to be clouds. These clouds were not like the ones that hold rain and snow. Although they looked like clouds, they were made of a straw-like substance.

As we descended to another level, I heard many noises—the sounds of eagles, wildebeests, seagulls, and bears, but no human sounds. Everywhere I looked, there was nothing but clouds set against the clearest white background. The noises grew louder as I descended. Finally, when I reached the ground, I saw creatures that must have been angels. It's extremely hard for me to describe the appearance of these incredible creatures. They weren't all in white apparel. The angels in my vision were dressed in several different colors, and I might add that color—yes, color—was the theme of this heavenly, angelic dream. I think I now understand why God went to such great lengths in Ezekiel 28 to explain Lucifer's covering, to give some clarity and information on what heaven was like and on the appearance of this creature.

The language of the angels seemed, to my human ears, to be a mixture of sounds made by different animals—like roaring, chirping, and hissing sounds combined with the noises from wildebeests, seagulls, and eagles. There were also sounds that I had never heard before.

There was a creature who looked like a man, with feet, hands, shoulders, and head. But when I looked closer at its head, it appeared to be composed of nothing but ears of different sizes. There was another creature with a man's body whose head was formed entirely of eyes—blue eyes, brown eyes, hazel eyes, green eyes—and the eyes were blinking. And I saw creatures flying from one side of heaven to the other; they all had several sets of wings, but appeared to have human bodies as well.

Though this may sound hideous, it was quite beautiful and fascinating. I don't know if this is how it is in heaven or whether God was simply showing me only what my human intellect could grasp. Then I saw the angel that had four faces—the faces of an ox, an eagle, a lion, and a man. When I beheld all this I remember saying, "I've read about this in the Bible."

And as two of those angels sped across the sky, I looked to see if they were holding a ring or a wheel like those described by Ezekiel. Although they moved across the open air in the heavenlies, they were not holding anything; they just moved about freely.

And then I woke up, fascinated by all that I had seen and heard.

## Day Two

The dream I had the next night seemed pretty strange. It was as if the Spirit of the Lord was narrating and navigating me through a recapitulation of what I had dreamed the night before. I went through the rainbows, through the different sounds, the music, the steps of colors, the abundance of gifts, and the home of those creatures who made strange noises.

And then He put me back on earth again. When I "landed," I was sitting in a church with which I'm extremely familiar. There were people praying for the baptism of the Holy Spirit, tarrying for the Holy Spirit to come down. As I looked near the altar, there I was, on my knees, praying and tarrying for the Holy Spirit, pleading with God for something He so willingly and freely gives to everyone who simply asks of Him. I was begging and, in the dream, I heard the Lord say, "Beg not, but only ask, and I shall give it unto you. So shall it be yours." I remember stopping and asking God for it and feeling the presence of the Lord so strongly that I woke up.

# The Dream: Seven Days in the Spirit

When I awakened, I wondered, "Am I hallucinating? Did I really just have a dream, or is this true?"

Later, when I went back to sleep, I returned to the altar in my dream where I saw myself begging, caught in somewhat of a tug-of-war. A young man in a suit approached me and said, "Let me show you the importance of receiving the baptism of the Holy Spirit." Suddenly I was standing in a completely white room without any furniture. The man stood before me and directed my attention to a balcony suspended over the entire earth. From the balcony I could see the principalities of Satan and a massive wall that Satan had erected around the entire earth. In every nook and cranny of the earth, he had demons, which were very frightening.

There were dark clouds and lightning hovering over the kingdom, as if there was an electric storm. And from under the satanic kingdom came a collection of beautiful lights in the form of blazing arrows, which traveled upward. "These are the prayers of the saints," an angel said.

I also saw disfigured creatures that were half-giraffe and half-elephant; half-woman and half-man; half-hyena and half-human. Everything was hideous and dysfunctional. It was as if an entire race had been annihilated and some Frankenstein had come to put it back together again, using bits and pieces from all over the earth. And the Spirit of the Lord told me, "These are demonic spirits who seek to embody men in the earth."

And that was it. I woke up. For an entire day I forgot the whole dream. Once I remembered, though, it frightened and quieted me. I was confused and excited, yet silent and still.

## Day Three

Two days passed before my third dream came. In this dream, I looked up and saw saints everywhere, all around the world, praying at the same time. The prayers, which exited their mouths in the form of mist, traveled through ceilings, through the roofs of their cars, and up into the heavenlies. All the prayers appeared on television screens in the heavens where Satan had demonic forces watching the prayers as if they were observing Dow-Jones or NASDAQ results from Wall Street. The demons put checks next to each prayer, signaling whether or not they were going to let the prayers be released to heaven.

And I saw a throne that was as white as snow and appeared to be pure. A man with white shoes, white socks, and white pants sat on this throne. I remember the pants were pressed so sharply that they could have cut someone. I did not see this man's face. I saw his head, though, and he had slicked-back, silken hair. His fingernails were well-manicured, and his right hand held three arrows.

The Spirit of the Lord said to me, "These arrows are the three musical spirits who have shaped modern culture." I beheld the arrows, and as I looked at them, physical heads appeared on each one: Boy George, Michael Jackson, and Prince, all entertainers who are unnaturally feminine in appearance and behavior. The arrows were given to a disfigured animal, a demonic spirit, who shot them at the earth in different directions. The arrows curved and turned, hit bull's-eyes, went through the bull's-eyes, and boomeranged back to the principalities, from where they were shot again. In the late 80s and early 90s, the music of Prince, Boy George, and Michael Jackson shaped the world. The arrows, upon hitting the bull's-eyes, released ungodly, off-key music, along with perversion, molestation, the stench of incest, and a number of other hideous spirits. The angel said, "As the culture changes, so shall the arrows change." And I propose to you today that there are demonic forces up in the heavens who now shoot the same arrows, only with the faces of different people of influence upon them.

After a while, I told my pastor about the series of dreams I was having and how I was not quite sure of what they meant. Thinking that perhaps the devil was disturbing my sleep, he prayed that I would not come under any further demonic attacks. However, when he related portions of my second dream in his sermon that next Sunday, our congregation erupted into a worshipful spirit that it had never quite experienced before. It was obvious that the message of my dream had the anointing of God upon it. The congregation burst into praise, and our morning service, which began at ten o'clock, didn't end until five o'clock that evening.

Excited with what God had done through the sharing of my dream, the pastor called me into his office to hear more. I can't explain what happened next except to say that at that very moment, the Lord took away the memory of my dreams. All I could tell the pastor was, "I'm sorry. I can't remember." For some reason the Lord wasn't ready for me to share any more at that time. Later, the memory of my dreams was restored, and the Lord led me to write them down. I can only pray that the movement of the Spirit that came upon the congregation that Sunday will be upon you as you read these words.

## Days Four and Five

After my talk with the pastor, I went home and prayed that God would give me understanding and guidance on what I was going through. Shortly thereafter I had my fourth dream.

In this dream, the same man who approached me while I was at the altar praying in dream two came to me again. This time he announced that he was a messenger of the Lord and that he was going to show me great things. I went to a window, opened it up, and found myself on the same balcony from my earlier dream. Under the balcony were the words, "Balcony of Ages." And the man, who was an angel, said to me, "Before you are all the generations, and these are the spirits who will attack those generations." And then he showed me a great cloud, which came in a rumble, like someone playing a thunderous drum roll. The angel said there was a mighty force who would combat the forces of evil, and I knew what that power was—the Holy Spirit who would come in a mighty rushing wind.

The angel then took me briefly back to dream three to show me the demons standing around the walls. Then he led me to Calvary. I heard the nails ringing and the hammers pounding—bang, bang, bang. The crowd screamed and hollered, but I didn't see Jesus. I knew in my spirit, though, that I was at Calvary.

Soon there was a calm. Then the peace was shattered by screeching that came from a violin. I heard noises and voices again, as if I were back in the chamber from dream one. And the messenger of the Lord turned and said, "This is the age I will raise up my army."

I then had a tremendous revelation on the valley of dry bones, which Ezekiel had seen in a vision in Old Testament times. In this revelation, which came from my dream during night five, God showed me the valley of dry bones and then connected it to Pentecost, the captivity of Judah, and the declaration of Israel as a nation.

So I was on the Balcony of Ages. I saw the ages to come and all the demonic arrows and spirits that were directed toward it. But I heard a rumbling in the open air, and I saw this cloud of glory on its way. And the proclamation from the messenger of God was that this is the power that will combat the forces of the enemy. In my dream, this Scripture came to me:

> And when the day of Pentecost was fully come, they were all with one accord in one place. And suddenly there came a sound from heaven as of a rushing mighty wind, and it filled all the house where they were sitting. And there appeared unto them cloven tongues like as of fire, and it sat upon each of them. And they were all filled with the Holy Ghost, and began to speak with other tongues, as the Spirit gave them utterance.        (Acts 2:1–4)

It dawned on me that my dreams started on the commemorated Day of Pentecost, Pentecost Sunday. I realized that God was revealing to me the purpose of Pentecost—the purpose of 120 individuals in the Upper Room, the purpose of the outpouring of the Spirit. He was revealing to me how dirty vessels will be made clean and how, through His blood, He would take dirty water and turn it into wine.

Scripture became so alive to me in my dreams that the rumbling of a great cloud beneath me became the moaning and groaning, the travailing of God in the Spirit, as He gave birth to the Holy Ghost on earth. He was waiting, though, for the 120 vessels to come together in one accord, in the same mind for a moment, so they could house His presence. He could then make His entrance onto the earth and combat the demonic forces of the ages that were eagerly waiting to attack the earth.

Through the propitiation and regeneration effected by the blood of the Lamb, the prophecy of a wedding at Cana had now come to pass on the Day of Pentecost. As recorded in the gospel of John, Jesus was invited to the wedding. When they ran out of wine, Jesus asked for six waterpots. These waterpots were nothing short of bathtubs where the people washed their feet after their long journeys on dusty roads. For the Scripture says, *"There were set there six waterpots of stone, after the manner of the purifying of the Jews, containing two or three firkins* [twenty to thirty gallons] *apiece"* (John 2:6). These pots were used for cleaning. And it was these— these dirty, dingy pots—that were brought to Jesus.

And He commanded them to be filled with water, representing life. Empty vessels were filled with water, life, the Spirit of God. The transforming power that took place at Pentecost was the same power Christ used when He turned water into wine. The Holy Spirit—pure, clean, and perfect—filled and transformed empty vessels, and He continues that work to this day.

# The Dream: Seven Days in the Spirit

As the ruler or governor of the feast at the wedding tasted the wine, he remarked that they had saved the best for last, but the Scripture says he did not know from where the wine had come. He did not realize that this wonderful wine had, just moments before, been ordinary water. The Holy Spirit is coming in the most fantastic and awesome way to renew our vessels, our spirits, just as Christ renewed the water jugs on that day.

There is yet another wind to blow, another groaning. For the Bible declares in Revelation 7:1–4 that there are angels standing on the four corners of the earth, holding back the four winds of the earth, that it shall not blow on any tree or on the land until God has sealed the foreheads of His servants. The number that he heard was 144,000, and that 144,000 represents Israel in connection to the tribulation period that is about to come. I understood all this on the fifth night of my dream.

## Day Six

About a week later, God took me back into the spirit realm. I was on the Balcony of Ages again, looking out over the earth as the saints prayed. On this night, though, my vision extended far beyond the Balcony of Ages. I was standing in the principalities and beholding the television screens, looking at the actual prayers of the saints as they reached the heavenlies. Moment by moment angels dropped down into the principalities, looking to the left and to the right and then falling down again to go into the earth. From time to time the angels would come out of heaven and into the principalities and look in both directions. But before they would make their next leap into the earthly realm, they would be snatched by demonic forces and held in a prison cell.

And the messenger of the Lord said to me, "This is the word of the Lord coming live to you now. Have I not told you all this in the book of Daniel?" And my spirit quickened in the dream as I remembered Daniel 10:13, which tells about Daniel's prayer getting detained by the prince of Persia for twenty-one days. And God had to release an angel to fight, while a host of angels in the heavenly realm prayed, warring with the demonic forces to release the prayers of God's people.

Though this sixth dream was short, it was very revelatory. On this night I began to understand that God often answers prayers as soon as we send them, but oftentimes His answers and His blessings are blocked by another force in the heavenly realm. The saints need only to have patience and faith, and to know this principle: If God's answer hasn't come, it will. Don't stop praising; don't stop praying; don't give up. Hold on because the angels of the Lord are wrestling for you.

## Day Seven

My seventh dream came twenty days after the first night of dreams. I remember thinking, "Oh, Lord, I'm dreaming again." I knew something was happening, but I wasn't sure what. I didn't know if it was a dream or if it was a vision. I saw an enormous cloud being released. Then the messenger of the Lord said to me, "We must go to Calvary." And so we went back to Calvary. Once again I heard the unbearably loud screaming, the yelling, and the ringing of the hammer. Amid the noise and confusion, voices shouted out, "Give us Barabbas! Give us Barabbas!" I heard roosters crowing and voices crying, "I don't know Him! I don't know Him!" There were many voices.

Then came the calm. The night changed to day as sunrise came. And there was violin music along with somber singing. I saw two women at the sepulchre; both were weeping and crying. And a messenger of the Lord said, "He is risen!"

This was love.

Then the scene changed and we were back on the Balcony of Ages. I looked down again and saw the cloud from before. It was now closer, and the sound from it was louder than before. There was wind with the cloud and something was going on around it really quickly. Lightning and flashing came out of it as it approached the balcony, and a whirlwind came out of it. Soon there was shaking and pieces of the building fell off.

Then, in the spirit realm, I saw everyone who was in the Upper Room. People were everywhere, filling the streets, and they were all speaking different languages. And everyone was reunited with his or her loved ones because there was an interpreter that wasn't there in times past. Peter stood up, saying, *"For these are not drunken, as ye suppose, seeing it is but the third hour of the day"* (Acts 2:15).

Then I looked up, and the messenger of the Lord said, "Behold, now: Satan's kingdom." And as I looked at Satan's kingdom and the principalities, there was mass confusion. Before, when the people prayed in their native languages, the demons had been able to write down what they said. On the Day of Pentecost, though, the saints stopped speaking their native tongues; they started speaking other tongues of men, and the door was opened for them to speak in the tongues of angels. And when they started praying in unknown tongues, the fallen angels could not unravel their prayers.

## Empowered from Above

And God revealed to me that He had sent the Holy Spirit not only to comfort us, lead us, and guide us into all truth, but also to stop Satan from interfering with and hindering our prayer life. If ever there was a time for the body of Christ to rise up and understand the unseen power of the Holy Spirit, the hidden mystery of speaking in unknown tongues as the Spirit of God gives utterance, this is that time. The time is now.

# Chapter One

---

# The Purpose of Pentecost

*In my dream, this Scripture came to me:*

> *And when the Day of Pentecost was fully come, they were all with one accord in one place. And suddenly there came a sound from heaven as of a rushing mighty wind, and it filled all the house where they were sitting. And there appeared unto them cloven tongues like as of fire, and it sat upon each of them. And they were all filled with the Holy Ghost, and began to speak with other tongues, as the Spirit gave them utterance.*          (Acts 2:1–4)

*It dawned on me that my dreams started on the commemorated Day of Pentecost, Pentecost Sunday. I realized that God was revealing to me the purpose of Pentecost—the purpose of 120 individuals in the Upper Room, the purpose of the outpouring of the Spirit. He was revealing to me how dirty vessels will be made clean and how, through His blood, He would take dirty water and turn it into wine.*

# Chapter One

# The Purpose of Pentecost

M any Christians sincerely hunger after a fuller, deeper experience of Christ, a hunger that stems from their desire to gain more knowledge of the Holy Spirit. It is on this path to receiving the indwelling of the Holy Spirit, however, that many believers become perplexed and confused about the baptism of the Holy Spirit. Though rarely dealt with, the indwelling of the Holy Spirit is an important topic, one closely related to the manifestation of the person of Jesus Christ; it deserves our full attention. The best place to start our learning journey is in Acts, where the Bible records the Holy Spirit's first indwelling of believers.

## Power in the Upper Room

Thousands of years ago in a place called the Upper Room, 120 men plus woman came together at the command of the Lord Jesus. There they anxiously waited to be endued with power from on high. It was somewhat of a prayer meeting experience, where a number of individuals waited for God to appear to them again.

It's important to note that the manifestation of the Holy Spirit didn't come until Jesus had already returned to the heavens. In Acts 1:9 the disciples watched Him ascend on a cloud, the vehicle for His exodus to the heavens: *"And when he had spoken these things, while they beheld, he was taken up; and a cloud received him out of their sight."* Shortly after this, two visitors dressed in white apparel reminded the disciples that Christ would come again: *"Ye men of Galilee, why stand ye gazing up into heaven? this same Jesus, which is taken up from you into heaven, shall so come in like manner as ye have seen him go into heaven"* (Acts 1:11). The disciples knew to expect a return of the Lord's presence.

In the Upper Room a number of things took place. First the congregation of the Lord assembled. They gathered together in unity of purpose. *"And when the day of Pentecost was fully come, they were all with one accord in one place"* (Acts 2:1). On the Day of Pentecost, the disciples, who believed Jesus' words and remained in Jerusalem to wait for His promise, were all together in one place. Even more significant, they were of one mind. This is a good reminder that some of us need to settle down, get in one place, set aside our differences, and let Pentecost fully come into our lives. Some people seek God so halfheartedly, without purposefulness, that they are completely unsure of His will for their lives. But God doesn't do a halfway job on anything. When God does something, He does it thoroughly and with expertise. We need to be expectant and unified in purpose as we wait for God to do His work in our lives.

Next in the Upper Room, the congregation prayed, as recorded in Acts 1:14: *"These all continued with one accord in prayer and supplication."* Don't miss the significance of what they did. In unity of spirit, they prayed and sought God. And finally they waited; they tarried for the Lord. They sat still until something spectacular and supernatural took place. It came upon them from above. In Acts 2, it happened; the baptism came. The baptism that took place in this room, however, was in no way comparable to the water baptism of John or even to our modern-day baptisms in the name of the Father, the Son, and the Holy Spirit. This baptism was a baptism from above, a baptism of fire, not of water. It wasn't the emergence into water; it wasn't the sprinkling; it was the indwelling of the Holy Spirit—the God-factor, who came to live within the temple of the hearts of individuals.

> *And suddenly there came a sound from heaven as of a rushing mighty wind, and it filled all the house where they were sitting. And there appeared unto them cloven tongues like as of fire, and it sat upon each of them. And they were all filled with the Holy Ghost, and began to speak with other tongues, as the Spirit gave them utterance.* (Acts 2:2–4)

As these seekers were earnestly asking and waiting, God provided two symbols of the Spirit's presence: the wind, which the Jews associated with the Holy Spirit—*"And suddenly there came a sound from heaven as of a rushing mighty wind, and it filled all the house where they were sitting"*— and fiery tongues, which divided and rested upon each one, showing that the Spirit's baptism included all—*"And there appeared unto them cloven tongues like as of fire, and it sat upon each of them."*

The Scripture then tells us that they were filled with the Holy Spirit and spoke in other tongues. *"And they were all filled with the Holy Ghost, and began to speak with other tongues, as the Spirit gave them utterance."* What does this mean? Does it mean the Christians at Pentecost began speaking like babies, practicing elementary babblings until they actually spoke something coherent? Or did they speak in other languages?

## Other Tongues

When the Bible declares here that these Christians spoke with other tongues, it means just that: They actually spoke other languages. Every man, regardless of his nationality, spoke in another language, witnessing to others and proclaiming the wonderful works of Christ. The "babble theory" is simply not scriptural, for the people who heard these Christians understood what they were saying. Why? Because each man heard his own tongue being spoken:

> *And they were all filled with the Holy Ghost, and began to speak with other tongues, as the Spirit gave them utterance. And there were dwelling at Jerusalem Jews, devout men, out of every nation under heaven. Now when this was noised abroad, the multitude came together, and were confounded, because that every man heard them speak in his own language.* (Acts 2:4–6)

## The Sign of Tongues

Now let's look at the purpose that tongues served at Pentecost. The purpose for the sign—the gift of tongues—was to get the attention of the unbelievers gathered there so that they would listen. Paul acknowledged this purpose

The Purpose of Pentecost

for tongues in 1 Corinthians 14:22: *"Wherefore tongues are for a sign, not to them that believe, but to them that believe not: but prophesying serveth not for them that believe not, but for them which believe."*

This certainly worked. All the different languages definitely caught the attention of those gathered there. They heard and saw things that they had never seen before, and they were astonished! How could these Galileans speak in so many different languages? Some even thought the apostles were drunk! Peter cleared up this misconception:

*For these are not drunken, as ye suppose, seeing it is but the third hour of the day. But this is that which was spoken by the prophet Joel; And it shall come to pass in the last days, saith God, I will pour out of my Spirit upon all flesh: and your sons and your daughters shall prophesy, and your young men shall see visions, and your old men shall dream dreams: and on my servants and on my handmaidens I will pour out in those days of my Spirit; and they shall prophesy: and I will show wonders in heaven above, and signs in the earth beneath; blood, and fire, and vapour of smoke: the sun shall be turned into darkness, and the moon into blood, before that great and notable day of the Lord come: and it shall come to pass, that whosoever shall call on the name of the Lord shall be saved.* (Acts 2:15–21)

Something awesome had happened. It wasn't a made-up show. In other tongues, these men of God spoke of His wonderful works. God showed up on the scene without anyone's help and filled them with the Holy Spirit, and they spoke in actual languages, in the known tongues of men.

When the Holy Spirit speaks to a group of people, He will reveal God's will in various ways. If He so chooses, He will give the one He fills the divine ability to speak in a human language foreign to that person, just as He did on the Day of Pentecost. If He chooses, He will reveal a message through an unknown tongue in a spiritual language and accompany it with the gift of interpretation.

## Prophecy: The "Other" Sign

Peter reminded us in his powerful message that tongues are not the only sign of the Holy Spirit's presence; prophecy is as well: *"And it shall come to pass in the last days, saith God, I will pour out of my Spirit upon all flesh: and your sons and your daughters shall prophesy"* (Acts 2:17). So often we focus on tongues but ignore prophecy as a sign of the gift of baptism in the Holy Spirit. Scripture reminds us, though, that both are signs of the Holy Spirit. When Paul laid his hands on the converts, they spoke in tongues *and* prophesied. *"And when Paul had laid his hands upon them, the Holy Ghost came on them; and they spake with tongues, and prophesied"* (Acts 19:6). When Peter stood up to preach on the Day of Pentecost, he prophesied through a stirring sermon that won 3,000 converts to Christ (see Acts 2:41); Peter understood that Joel's prophecy was not completely fulfilled but only just beginning at that feast.

As that prophecy continues to be fulfilled today, we are going to experience an outpouring of the Spirit as never before. People who have never spoken English will speak English without learning it; others will speak in Russian, Greek, Hebrew, Chinese, Japanese—all kinds of tongues—without learning them. Unity in the body of Christ is also going to come. Thousands of people are going to be saved, and denominational differences will be set aside!

So whether the Holy Spirit works through actual human languages or through the heavenly language of angels, He won't speak to a group of people in a language they can't understand. This is why He gave explicit instructions through His anointed minister concerning the use of tongues:

> *If any man speak in an unknown tongue, let it be by two, or at the most by three, and that by course; and let one interpret. But if there be no interpreter, let him keep silence in the church; and let him speak to himself, and to God.*
>
> (1 Corinthians 14:27–28)

Earlier in this same chapter Paul acknowledged the importance of ensuring God's order in the congregation through intelligent, understandable speech while also acknowledging the place of prophecy and private tongues for the purpose of revelation and edification:

> *For he that speaketh in an unknown tongue speaketh not unto men, but unto God: for no man understandeth him; howbeit in the spirit he speaketh mysteries. But he that prophesieth speaketh unto men to edification, and exhortation, and comfort. He that speaketh in an unknown tongue edifieth himself; but he that prophesieth edifieth the church.*

# Empowered from Above

*I would that ye all spake with tongues, but rather that ye prophesied: for greater is he that prophesieth than he that speaketh with tongues, except he interpret, that the church may receive edifying.*

(1 Corinthians 14:2–5)

So Paul encouraged every Christian to speak in tongues, but only according to God's instructions. Notice what is happening in some churches today with regard to speaking in tongues, and consider whether it is done in the Spirit or the flesh. Many today are trying to be popular in religious circles instead of living and walking in the Spirit. Sister and Brother So-and-So might speak out in tongues they should have kept to themselves because they received no inspiration to move in the gift of congregational tongues with the interpretation mentioned in 1 Corinthians 12:

*And God hath set some in the church, first apostles, secondarily prophets, thirdly teachers, after that miracles, then gifts of healings, helps, governments, diversities of tongues. Are all apostles? are all prophets? are all teachers? are all workers of miracles? Have all the gifts of healing? do all speak with tongues? do all interpret?* (vv. 28–30)

At worst, some speak in tongues merely to draw attention to themselves. There is no special revelation, no anointing, and sometimes these tongues even interfere with what the Holy Spirit actually wants to do.

On the Day of Pentecost, God chose to speak to the nations gathered there in each one's own language, as a sign to unbelievers of His presence on earth. His presence was confirmed through the symbolic signs of fire and wind, as well as through prophecy. From that day on the Spirit has continued to manifest Himself in various gifts of His own distribution. Through discernible speech and gifts, God's people can be intelligently instructed about His redemptive plans and purposes.

This is what really happened on the Day of Pentecost.

# Chapter Two

## Who Is This Holy Spirit?

*And God revealed to me that He had sent the Holy Spirit not only to comfort us, lead us, and guide us into all truth, but also to stop Satan from interfering with and hindering our prayer life. If ever there was a time for the body of Christ to rise up and understand the unseen power of the Holy Spirit, the hidden mystery of speaking in unknown tongues as the Spirit of God gives utterance, this is that time. The time is now.*

# Chapter Two

# Who Is This Holy Spirit?

*But the Comforter, which is the Holy Ghost, whom the*
*Father will send in my name, he shall teach you all things,*
*and bring all things to your remembrance, whatsoever*
*I have said unto you.*
—John 14:26

So, who is the Holy Spirit? Who is this Person who came on the Day of Pentecost? What is He like? Praise God He has not left us without answers to these questions! Praise Him that He has revealed to us the Holy Spirit through His most perfect and precious Word!

## In the Beginning

*And the earth was without form, and void; and dark-*
*ness was upon the face of the deep. And the Spirit*
*of God moved upon the face of the waters....And the*
*LORD God formed man of the dust of the ground, and*
*breathed into his nostrils the breath of life; and man*
*became a living soul.* (Genesis 1:2; 2:7)

# Empowered from Above

The Holy Spirit was with God from the start. As Genesis shows, the Holy Spirit was God's agent of creation, the breath of life from God into man. This beautifully mysterious nature of God is one of the most awesome and inexplicable revelations of the Bible: God in three persons—blessed Trinity! God the Father, God the Son, and God the Holy Spirit: They are one. This is hard for us to fathom. Three separate persons, united in one great Trinity. We must never try to separate the Three: The Father, the Son, and the Holy Spirit. They are one and have been so, all the way from time's beginning.

> *In the beginning God created the heaven and the earth. And the earth was without form, and void; and darkness was upon the face of the deep. And the Spirit of God moved upon the face of the waters....And God said, Let **us** make man in **our** image, after **our** likeness.*
> (Genesis 1:1–2, 26, emphasis added)

Notice that God said, *"Let us,"* implying the presence of more than one Person in the Godhead. But how can this be? How can three persons be one? This is one of the many paradoxes, or mysteries, of Christianity. One way to understand it a little better is to think about water. Water is water, no matter what form it's in. It can be the liquid you shower in every night, the steam that comes out of your teapot, or the ice cubes you put in your orange juice every morning. Just as there are three separate forms of water, there are three separate persons in the Trinity. And just as all three forms of water are one hundred percent water, so too all persons of the Trinity are one hundred percent God. We may not completely understand it, but it's true. It's one of those things we just have to leave to faith.

# Who Is This Holy Spirit?

Back to the beginning: In the beginning Adam was just a form—until God breathed life into him, until He breathed His Spirit into Adam's shell. Only then did he become a living soul. The Holy Spirit is God's life-giving wind, or breath.

As a descendant of Adam, you also are just a form until God breathes life into your nostrils. Physically alive, you might run, walk, talk, get dressed in the morning, go to work, hop on the bus to head for school—but you are just going through the motions until the Holy Spirit breathes His life into you. Until then, you are a mere form, bodily alive but not really living in the fullness of the Spirit.

How is this so? Because without the Spirit, you are spiritually dead. When Adam sinned, He died spiritually; consequently, all his descendants were born spiritually dead as well. Without the breath of God, or the Holy Spirit, you are spiritually dead; you don't have the power to understand your origin, your purpose, your spiritual identity.

After Christ returned to heaven, though, He sent *"another Comforter"* (John 14:16)—His Holy Spirit. Those who acknowledge Jesus as Savior and submit to the Trinity's working in their lives receive this Spirit. And, beginning with this new birth re-creation, through the empowering of human beings with supernatural gifts, the Holy Spirit gives the power and ability to do the things God has ordained His children to do.

The Bible is clear; outside of Him, there is no life:

*But ye are not in the flesh, but in the Spirit, if so be that the Spirit of God dwell in you. Now if any man have not the Spirit of Christ, he is none of his.*
(Romans 8:9)

# Empowered from Above

Without the Spirit, we have no life. He is our Source, our spiritual Breath.

He is our Comforter, Teacher, and powerful Helper. He is here to assist us in our Christian walk with God. He is here to help us even when we don't know how we—or someone we are praying for—can best be helped:

> *Likewise the Spirit also helpeth our infirmities: for we know not what we should pray for as we ought: but the Spirit itself maketh intercession for us with groanings which cannot be uttered.* (Romans 8:26)

He is the Spirit of God who dwells inside those who receive Jesus Christ as Savior and Lord, and He abides with us forever because He is eternal. He is abiding in you right now if you have asked Him into your heart. So keep on reading to learn more of what all this actually means.

## He Shall Teach You

Just as Jesus taught the disciples during His time here on earth, so too does the Holy Spirit guide and teach those who belong to Him. Jesus said in John 14:26,

> *But the Comforter, which is the Holy Ghost, whom the Father will send in my name, he shall teach you all things, and bring all things to your remembrance, whatsoever I have said unto you.*

The Holy Spirit works as a Guide, reminding us of the things Jesus has taught, encouraging us to follow in those ways.

The purpose of the Holy Spirit in your life is to teach you His truths and help you accomplish the things God has called you to do. Oftentimes He convicts us of sin or convinces us of certain actions we must take. So there really is no reason for someone who has the Holy Spirit not to know the truth.

When people who have the Holy Spirit find themselves beginning to be drawn toward activities that are contrary to God's Word, if they are sensitive to the Spirit's voice, they know that they are heading in the wrong direction. His presence within cautions them and they stop what they are doing; the Holy Spirit has convicted them that what they are doing is wrong. Praise God, though, that He uses our troubled consciences—this "thorn in the flesh"—for His glory and our good. Such thorns drive us to Him for deliverance from sin and keep us humble enough to have patience with others who experience the same sort of struggles. Paul explained it best:

> But I keep under my body, and bring it into subjection: lest that by any means, when I have preached to others, I myself should be a castaway.
>
> (1 Corinthians 9:27)

Paul understood that without keeping himself subjected to the anointing of the Holy Spirit, where he could have a continued cleansing and deliverance, he'd be preaching deliverance to others while he remained bound.

## Another Comforter

The Holy Spirit is not only a Convicter; He is a Comforter. Jesus described Him in this way in several passages recorded by John. We read:

*But the Comforter, which is the Holy Ghost, whom the Father will send in my name, he shall teach you all things, and bring all things to your remembrance, whatsoever I have said unto you.* (John 14:26)

*But when the Comforter is come, whom I will send unto you from the Father, even the Spirit of truth, which proceedeth from the Father, he shall testify of me: and ye also shall bear witness, because ye have been with me from the beginning.*
(John 15:26–27)

*Nevertheless I tell you the truth; It is expedient for you that I go away: for if I go not away, the Comforter will not come unto you; but if I depart, I will send him unto you.* (John 16:7)

Scripture also refers to the Holy Spirit as *another* Comforter, in fact, meaning He is a Comforter just as Jesus was a Comforter.

*And I will pray the Father, and he shall give you another Comforter, that he may abide with you for ever; even the Spirit of truth; whom the world cannot receive, because it seeth him not, neither knoweth him: but ye know him; for he dwelleth with you, and shall be in you.* (John 14:16–17)

You probably have an idea of what the word *comforter* means. One definition of *comforter* is "a thick bed covering made of two layers of cloth containing a filling." We all know what this kind of comforter is. On a cold rainy day, or on a day when we're feeling tired and under the weather, nothing sounds as good as curling up in bed underneath a big, fluffy comforter. It warms us up and makes us feel better; it comforts us.

But even the softest blanket cannot compare to the comforting of the Holy Spirit. For when we talk about the Holy Spirit, the word *Comforter* means "helper; one who comforts." In this passage we just read, Jesus had told His disciples He was returning to the Father but that the Comforter, whom the Father would send in Jesus' name, would abide with them forever. Not only would He embrace them, console them, and make them feel better; He would help them, guide them, and lead them in truth and wisdom. Jesus said the Holy Spirit, the Spirit of Truth, would teach and bring to the disciples' remembrance all those things Christ taught during His time on earth. Jesus encouraged the disciples by assuring them that the Comforter would be with them. And that is why the Holy Spirit is sent to you: to come alongside you, to help you understand Jesus' teachings, and to enable you to do God's work.

You see, He's not just about giving hugs when you're sad. He is your Teacher, your personal Trainer, your Encourager, your Discipler. Don't ever fall into the trap of believing He is *your* assistant to help you carry out *your* plans. Rather, the indwelling presence of the Holy Spirit is there to assist you in becoming more Christlike, to encourage you along the path of righteousness, and to equip you to be about your Father's business. (See Luke 2:49.)

# Chapter Three

# Why Tongues?

*The* angels in my vision were dressed in several different colors, and I might add that color—yes, color—was the theme of this heavenly, angelic dream. I think I now understand why God went to such great lengths in Ezekiel 28 to explain Lucifer's covering, to give some clarity and information on what heaven was like and on the appearance of this creature.

*The* language of the angels seemed, to my human ears, to be a mixture of sounds made by different animals—like roaring, chirping, and hissing sounds combined with the noises from wildebeests, seagulls, and eagles. There were also sounds that I had never heard before.

*There* was a creature who looked like a man, with feet, hands, shoulders, and head. But when I looked closer at its head, it appeared to be composed of nothing but ears of different sizes. There was another creature with a man's body whose head was formed entirely of eyes—blue eyes, brown eyes, hazel eyes, green eyes—and the eyes were blinking. And I saw creatures flying from one side of heaven to the other; they all had several sets of wings, but appeared to have human bodies as well.

*T*hough this may sound hideous, it was quite beautiful and fascinating. I don't know if this is how it is in heaven or whether God was simply showing me only what my human intellect could grasp. Then I saw the angel that had four faces—the faces of an ox, an eagle, a lion, and a man. When I beheld all this I remember saying, "I've read about this in the Bible."

*A*nd as two of those angels sped across the sky, I looked to see if they were holding a ring or a wheel like those described by Ezekiel. Although they moved across the open air in the heavenlies, they were not holding anything; they just moved about freely.

*A*nd then I woke up, fascinated by all that I had seen and heard.

# Chapter Three

# Why Tongues?

I remember growing up in the church as a young boy, struggling with my understanding of the gift of tongues. Having been raised in a Seventh-day Adventist church, I found it especially difficult to comprehend this unusual means of communicating with God. I had no understanding of the charismatic experience, and the idea of speaking in tongues only left me dumbfounded. How could anything of this nature usher anyone into the heavens, into spiritual and intimate conversation with God Almighty Himself?

After I was saved and converted to Pentecostalism, however, I found out that salvation was not enough. I longed for a deeper power to fill the void within whenever my initial zeal had ceased. Jesus said, *"Ask, and it shall be given you; seek, and ye shall find; knock, and it shall be opened unto you"* (Matthew 7:7). So I did just that; I was baptized with water, then received the baptism of the Holy Spirit, and immediately the experience of tongues came to me.

Speaking in tongues, however, is not to be confused with the initial evidence of being filled with the Holy Spirit. To imply that a person is not filled with the Holy Spirit because he or she does not speak in tongues is unsound teaching. Nowhere does the Bible say that speaking in tongues is the initial evidence of the Holy Spirit; instead, it continually talks about being endued with power from on high.

## Power from On High

The only clear spiritual evidence of baptism in the Holy Spirit is the endowment of power:

> *But ye shall receive power, after that the Holy Ghost is come upon you: and ye shall be witnesses unto me both in Jerusalem, and in all Judaea, and in Samaria, and unto the uttermost part of the earth.*
>
> (Acts 1:8)

Notice, the Word of God says that you *"shall receive power,"* not you "shall speak in tongues."

Five times in the book of Acts, the "tongue experience" is mentioned; in three of these times people spoke in tongues after being endued with power from on high. If three times they spoke in tongues after receiving power from on high and two times they did *not* speak in tongues after receiving power from on high, this alone discredits the statement that speaking in tongues is the initial and only evidence of being filled with the Holy Spirit.

I do not dispute, however, the teaching of tongues; several times in Scripture tongues are given as evidence of the Holy Spirit's filling. First and foremost, though, we must remember that endowment with power is the true mark of the Holy Spirit.

## Other Tongues

The Bible talks about two types of tongues: 1) other tongues or diversity of tongues and 2) unknown tongues or tongues of angels.

The gift of *other* tongues, which first took place at Pentecost, is the speaking of foreign languages by someone who has not been trained in that language. At Pentecost, it served as an experience for winning Jews to God.

*And when the day of Pentecost was fully come, they were all with one accord in one place. And suddenly there came a sound from heaven as of a rushing mighty wind, and it filled all the house where they were sitting. And there appeared unto them cloven tongues like as of fire, and it sat upon each of them. And they were all filled with the Holy Ghost, and began to speak with **other** tongues, as the Spirit gave them the utterance.*

(Acts 2:1–4, emphasis added)

Because this event at Pentecost is sometimes mistaken as the initial evidence of the Holy Spirit, people who do not manifest the Holy Spirit through tongues are often accused of not having the Holy Spirit. Remember, though, the universal evidence of the Holy Spirit is power from on high, not the ability to speak in tongues. A look at the sequence of events in Acts clarifies this fact. Here's how: Acts 1:8 says that the initial evidence of the Holy Spirit is the power to be a witness unto Christ. All believers, through the

Holy Spirit, shall be His witnesses, having the power necessary for properly communicating Christ to the world around them.

> *But ye shall receive power, after that the Holy Ghost is come upon you: and ye shall be witnesses unto me both in Jerusalem, and in all Judaea, and in Samaria, and unto the uttermost part of the earth.*
> (Acts 1:8)

Here Christ's emphasis is on the witnessing, not on speaking in tongues. Acts 2:4, which records events happening after Acts 1:8, says that they *"began to speak with other tongues, as the Spirit gave them utterance."* In other words, they began speaking in tongues after the Spirit enabled them, or revealed to them what to say. The key point, though, is that they were sharing Christ; the tongues were a tool for this witnessing. As they began to speak, men heard the wonderful works of God, and five thousand were added to the church.

Whenever there is an endowment of the Holy Spirit, the next step is sharing with someone the wonderful works of God through witnessing. Scripture is clear: The initial evidence of the Holy Spirit is the ability to witness and reveal to others God's magnificent power. When Jesus asked Peter, *"Whom say ye that I am?"* (see Matthew 16:15; Mark 8:29; Luke 9:20), Peter answered, *"Thou art the Christ, the Son of the living God"* (Matthew 16:16). Jesus then commended Peter because He knew Peter did not receive this revelation through his own intuitive knowledge; He assured Peter that it was revealed to him by the Spirit: *"Blessed art thou, Simon Barjona: for flesh and*

# Why Tongues?

*blood hath not revealed it unto thee, but my Father which is in heaven"* (Matthew 16:17). Once again, we see that the evidence of the Holy Spirit is receiving understanding and power from on high.

## The Experience of a Lifetime

During a crusade in Tanzania, Africa, I was privileged to experience the gift of tongues for about four solid minutes. During this time I began speaking in tongues and praying in the Spirit until I suddenly realized there was a great commotion in the audience.

The open field where we were holding the crusade contained about sixty to seventy thousand Tanzanians who had come to hear the message. Some had walked for six weeks to get to the field where I would preach the Word for eight nights straight. After my anointing began to lift, I stood before the people and began singing a song. I noticed there were thousands of people moving toward the front of the platform. Since I wasn't familiar with the type of services the Tanzanians were accustomed to, I asked my interpreter what was going on. He immediately told me that I had delivered a complete salvation message to these people of Tanzania, entirely in their native language. I, of course, did not know the native language of the Tanzanians; I know without a doubt that this was a divine orchestration of the Lord Jesus Christ.

This was one of the most powerful experiences of my ministerial career, not because of any great thing I had done but because of the awesome and miraculous power of the Father who carried out such an incredible feat. What a great honor it is to be used by the Lord!

## Unknown Tongues

In addition to *other tongues*, we want to deal with *unknown tongues*.

> *For he that speaketh in an unknown tongue speaketh not unto men, but unto God: for no man understandeth him; howbeit in the spirit he speaketh mysteries.*
> (1 Corinthians 14:2)

The Bible also refers to these as *"the tongues...of angels."*

> *Though I speak with the tongues of men and of angels, and have not charity, I am become as sounding brass, or a tinkling cymbal.*
> (1 Corinthians 13:1)

*"The tongues of men"* that Paul mentioned here are the various languages that he spoke, such as Greek, Roman, and Hebrew. When he referred to *"the tongues...of angels,"* though, he was not talking about the other tongues or diversity of tongues from 1 Corinthians 14:11. He was referring instead to unknown tongues.

When I pray in an unknown tongue, *"my spirit prayeth, but my understanding is unfruitful"* (1 Corinthians 14:14). These are the tongues used to unravel prophecy, the tongues used to pray in the expressed will of God, and the tongues used by the Holy Spirit to pray through us and articulate the language of heaven so that our needs are met. One must understand that the language of heaven is not French; nor is it Chinese, Spanish, English, Hebrew, or Greek. The language of heaven is a language unto itself. It can be spoken only through the supernatural phenomenon of the Holy Spirit. And when it's spoken, a supernatural manifestation is released. This is where God, without human intellectual assistance, gives us the power to pray in the will of the Father.

> *Howbeit when he, the Spirit of truth, is come, he will guide you into all truth: for he shall not speak of himself; but whatsoever he shall hear, that shall he speak: and he will show you things to come.*
> (John 16:13)

As Jesus said here, the Spirit speaks to us in a heavenly tongue, a tongue of the Father. This is above and beyond the reasoning of men.

## Tongues Are Good for You

Now that you know what really happened on the Day of Pentecost, you need to know that Pentecost is still happening today.

James wrote, *"Every good gift and every perfect gift is from above, and cometh down from the Father of lights, with whom is no variableness, neither shadow of turning"* (James 1:17). Because God is good and does not change, we can conclude that His gift of tongues is for today as well as for yesterday. Tongues, like *"every good...and...perfect gift,"* are still very good. They provide us with understanding, edification, a tool for praising God, and a sign of God's presence.

### Understanding: It Is Good to Know

Tongues are good because of the spiritual revelation they can provide to the Christian who seeks to know God intimately:

# Empowered from Above

*For he that speaketh in an unknown tongue speaketh*
*not unto men, but unto God: for no man understand-*
*eth him; howbeit in the spirit he speaketh mysteries.*
(1 Corinthians 14:2)

This word *"mysteries"* actually means "mouth-guarded, or concealed." So tongues are good because, whenever the language of the Holy Spirit is spoken, His mysteries are revealed so that we can better understand His ways.

Later in this chapter, Paul added that when we pray in an unknown tongue, *"[our] spirit prayeth, but [our] understanding is unfruitful"* (v. 14). In other words, Paul said that praying in tongues is good because the spirit prays—and if anybody knows what to say, the Spirit in us certainly does.

Paul encouraged us to pray so that we may hear the mysteries the Spirit speaks—and also interpret them. I would personally not want to speak a blessing in another language without understanding what that blessing was. If I was able to interpret it, though, I would be excited and edified. The experience of speaking in tongues is therefore nothing to be afraid of; we should not run from it or refuse to talk about it. Paul encouraged us to pray in both our known languages and in the Spirit's language. As we tune in to the Spirit's voice and cultivate our understanding, we will grow in wisdom and knowledge of God. And this is good.

*What is it then? I will pray with the spirit, and I will*
*pray with the understanding also: I will sing with*
*the spirit, and I will sing with the understanding also.*
(v. 15)

# Why Tongues?

## Edification: It Is Good to Grow

Paul said in 1 Corinthians 14:4, *"He that speaketh in an unknown tongue edifieth himself."* This word, *edify,* means "to build up." So tongues are also good because they build up, or strengthen, our Christian experience. True, the gift is not for the building up of the church unless an interpretation is provided. But even when there is no interpretation, tongues can be edifying in your personal fellowship with the Lord. When you pray in tongues privately, you are building up yourself, edifying your spirit—and that can only be good.

Paul's lengthy teaching in 1 Corinthians 14 was necessary because the Corinthians were so excited about their gift that they were speaking out constantly, without the anointing to speak in public tongues. This was causing confusion, and Paul had to set them in order. When interpretation is provided for a public speaking of tongues, the entire body can be edified.

## Tool for Praise: It Is Good to Worship the Lord

The gift of tongues is also good because it gives us the freedom and ability to more adequately praise God. Once again, though, Paul cautioned about the need for order when worshipping in a congregational setting because of the potential of confusing others who can't enter in:

> *Else when thou shalt bless with the spirit, how shall he that occupieth the room of the unlearned say Amen at thy giving of thanks, seeing he understandeth not what thou sayest? For thou verily givest thanks well, but the other is not edified.*
>
> (1 Corinthians 14:16–17)

# Empowered from Above

To help maintain order during times of public worship, Paul laid down God's guidelines for the use of tongues for praise:

> *I thank my God, I speak with tongues more than ye all: yet in the church I had rather speak five words with my understanding, that by my voice I might teach others also, than ten thousand words in an unknown tongue....How is it then, brethren? when ye come together, every one of you hath a psalm, hath a doctrine, hath a tongue, hath a revelation, hath an interpretation. Let all things be done unto edifying. If any man speak in an unknown tongue, let it be by two, or at the most by three, and that by course; and let one interpret. But if there be no interpreter, let him keep silence in the church; and let him speak to himself, and to God. Let the prophets speak two or three, and let the other judge. If any thing be revealed to another that sitteth by, let the first hold his peace. For ye may all prophesy one by one, that all may learn, and all may be comforted. And the spirits of the prophets are subject to the prophets. For God is not the author of confusion, but of peace, as in all churches of the saints.*
>
> (1 Corinthians 14:18–19, 26–33)

God intended tongues as a spiritual gift to assist in praising Him; as this passage points out, though, we must always use the gifts in an orderly fashion.

## Sign of God: It Is Good to See the Lord

Tongues are also good because of the supernatural sign they provide; they point unbelievers to the reality of God.

# Why Tongues?

We see this throughout Scripture; occurrences of tongues mentioned in Acts include Pentecost, the first Gentile outpouring in Acts 10, and Paul's ministry to the Ephesian men in Acts 19.

Putting these three events together, we first see that God gave tongues as a sign to the unsaved Jews in Jerusalem to confirm the message of the apostles. At the home of the Roman centurion, Cornelius, we see that tongues served as a sign to the Jews gathered, showing them that non-Jews could be saved. And then we see tongues manifested in the distant regions of Asia Minor for the personal edification and spiritual benefit of the speakers themselves. And all this was good.

Paul's ministry to the followers of John the Baptist in Ephesus also showed that the message of repentance is incomplete without the baptism of the Holy Spirit. This should serve as a witness to many denominations today that say speaking in tongues has passed away. Many congregations preach, "Just believe." Receiving after believing, however, is really the key, as these passages in Acts show us. If there are any pastors reading this who have resisted teaching the reality of the Holy Spirit's gift, start telling your congregation about the Holy Spirit and about how important it is to be filled with Him. He just might make tongues a sign to the unbelievers in your midst—you included—and this is good!

## Speaking in Tongues Is Not the "Super-Saint" Gift

*I would that ye all spake with tongues, but rather that ye prophesied: for greater is he that prophesieth than*

# Empowered from Above

*he that speaketh with tongues, except he interpret,*
*that the church may receive edifying.*

(1 Corinthians 14:5)

In our discussion on tongues, we need to address a common misconception. Although tongues are good, their use or nonuse is certainly no measure of the spiritual superiority or inferiority of God's people in the church. In 1 Corinthians 14:5, Paul essentially said, "It is good that you can speak in tongues, but you aren't a super-saint because of it; you aren't spiritually superior or special because you have the gift of tongues." He went on to say that, unless an interpreter is present whenever a message is publicly spoken in tongues, the one who prophesies is greater than the one who speaks in tongues without the message being interpreted.

So if people want to be "super-saints," they need to allow the gift of prophecy to work in them for the building up of the church. And, as I pointed out earlier in our discussion of the Day of Pentecost, this gift includes life-changing preaching.

# Chapter Four

## Receiving the Gift

*T*he dream I had the next night seemed pretty strange. It was as if the Spirit of the Lord was narrating and navigating me through a recapitulation of what I had dreamed the night before. I went through the rainbows, through the different sounds, the music, the steps of colors, the abundance of gifts, and the home of those creatures who made strange noises.

*A*nd then He put me back on earth again. When I "landed," I was sitting in a church with which I'm extremely familiar. There were people praying for the baptism of the Holy Spirit, tarrying for the Holy Ghost to come down. As I looked near the altar, there I was, on my knees, praying and tarrying for the Holy Ghost, pleading with God for something He so willingly and freely gives to everyone who simply asks of Him. I was begging and, in the dream, I heard the Lord say, "Beg not, but only ask, and I shall give it unto you. So shall it be yours." I remember stopping and asking God for it and feeling the presence of the Lord so strongly that I woke up. When I awakened, I wondered, "Am I hallucinating? Did I really just have a dream, or is this true?"

# Chapter Four

# Receiving the Gift

———————◆———◆———◆———————

B efore we consider the question of how to receive the Holy Spirit, let's take one more look at the practice of tongues, because the church has been confused on this issue for many years. Some ministers have taught false doctrines concerning tongues, sometimes going so far as to say that those who don't speak in tongues will go to hell. Such people believe that speaking in tongues is a salvation commandment from the Lord, and they actually scare people into believing their theory. Such teaching, however, is totally false; it is a lie from the devil.

## Tongues: A Gift — Not a Command

Once again, let's go to Paul for further truth on the subject of tongues, a topic that can be divisive if we do not have God's Word as the basis for our beliefs and doctrinal positions. Paul started his teaching on the Holy Spirit's gifts in 1 Corinthians 12:1: *"Now concerning spiritual gifts, brethren, I would not have you ignorant."* Paul took away our ignorance by telling us exactly what the spiritual gifts are:

*But the manifestation of the Spirit is given to every man to profit withal. For to one is given by the Spirit the word of wisdom; to another the word of knowledge by the same Spirit; to another faith by the same Spirit; to another the gifts of healing by the same Spirit; to another the working of miracles; to another prophecy; to another discerning of spirits; to another divers kinds of tongues; to another the interpretation of tongues: but all these worketh that one and the selfsame Spirit, dividing to every man severally as he will.* (1 Corinthians 12:7–11)

Notice what Paul said: Not everybody is given the same gift. The Holy Spirit distributes the gifts as He chooses, giving to each person his or her own unique set of gifts. One thing is always certain, though: The manifestation of the Spirit is given to profit everyone. The gifts will always be for the edification of the body of Christ. We are not commanded to do anything except to *"desire spiritual gifts"* (1 Corinthians 14:1). In other words, it's not our job to seek after particular gifts; the Holy Spirit makes that decision. He decides who gets what. Our job is simply to *"desire."*

Now look at the following passage from 1 Corinthians 12:

*Now ye are the body of Christ, and members in particular. And God hath set some in the church, first apostles, secondarily prophets, thirdly teachers, after that miracles, then gifts of healings, helps, governments, diversities of tongues. Are all apostles? are all prophets? are all teachers?*

*are all workers of miracles? Have all the gifts of healing? do all speak with tongues? do all interpret?*
(1 Corinthians 12:27–30)

In this passage, which speaks about public, congregational gifts, Paul emphasized the fact that God has set certain public ministries within the church. Note again, though, that everybody does not have the same gift; the Spirit gives the gift of healings to one person, the gift of tongues to another, and the gift of miracles to yet another. Every member will not be given every gift. So if your theory says that everybody must speak in tongues when the church assembles—or even that there *must* be a message in tongues every time the church assembles—then you have missed the meaning of Paul's teaching here. The Spirit manifests Himself through various gifts, *as He wills.*

So not everyone will receive the gift of tongues. Scripture is clear, though, that we are all to desire the Spirit and His gifts, whatever He chooses them to be. Remember Paul's words: *"Even so ye, forasmuch as ye are zealous of spiritual gifts, seek that ye may excel to the edifying of the church"* (1 Corinthians 14:12).

Now why did Paul teach the church to be zealous of spiritual gifts if the Holy Spirit distributes the gifts as He chooses? Because He opens the door to those who knock, ask, and seek—remember? And the Holy Spirit wants to give gifts—the gifts that He determines—to those who eagerly desire them. Paul continued by instructing the church to be people of prayer, both in tongues and in human language, thus giving the Spirit freedom to edify the church:

*For if I pray in an unknown tongue, my spirit prayeth, but my understanding is unfruitful. What is it then? I will pray with the spirit, and I will pray with the understanding also: I will sing with the spirit, and I will sing with the understanding also. Else when thou shalt bless with the spirit, how shall he that occupieth the room of the unlearned say Amen at thy giving of thanks, seeing he understandeth not what thou sayest? For thou verily givest thanks well, but the other is not edified.*

(1 Corinthians 14:14–17)

As we see from these Scriptures, the Spirit gives to certain ones the congregational gift of diversity of tongues; He commands no one to have it, however. What *is* commanded is repentance, baptism in the name of the Lord, and filling with the Holy Spirit. (See Acts 2:38; 10:48; 17:30.) And uniting all of these is love. (See John 13:34; 1 John 4:7.) We'll talk more about love in the next chapter.

## How to Receive

Now let's look into the realities of receiving the Holy Spirit and clear up some of the confusing doctrines that have kept many from experiencing His fullness. Many formulas and rituals have clouded and confounded the simple act of inviting the Holy Spirit into our hearts. He is waiting for us to respond to His call by repenting of our sins and receiving Him into our lives. Receiving Him doesn't have to be a complex process.

*Then Peter said unto them, Repent, and be baptized every one of you in the name of Jesus Christ for the remission of sins, and ye shall receive the gift of the Holy Ghost. For the promise is unto you, and to your children, and to all that are afar off, even as many as the Lord our God shall call.*

(Acts 2:38–39)

*For every one that asketh receiveth; and he that seeketh findeth; and to him that knocketh it shall be opened. Or what man is there of you, whom if his son ask bread, will he give him a stone? Or if he ask a fish, will he give him a serpent? If ye then, being evil, know how to give good gifts unto your children, how much more shall your Father which is in heaven give good things to them that ask him?*

(Matthew 7:8–11)

To *receive* something is "to take it into one's possession." When someone gives you a gift, do you respond by denying it? No, you take it. You receive it. And you're glad about receiving it. And when you receive that gift, it immediately becomes your possession. Why? Because it has been given to you.

In the same way, after you have accepted Christ as your Savior, you don't have to tarry or wait to be filled with the Holy Spirit—God's gift from above. As Peter preached in Acts 2:39, *"The promise is unto you, and to your children, and to all that are afar off, even as many as the Lord our God shall call."* God has called all those who will to receive His gift. So why wait to receive it into your possession?

As a young Christian from the streets of Brooklyn, New York, I was excited about my new life, enthusiastic and ready to receive all that the Lord had promised me as an inheritance. Soon after giving my life to the Lord, I was filled with the Holy Spirit, which, along with the Word of God, liberated me from a life of drug abuse, oppression, and bondage. It wasn't tarrying at the altar or the laying on of hands that filled me with the Spirit and set me free; it was simply faith, asking to receive what God had promised.

# No Need to Tarry!

The devil wants you to wait, to tarry, so he can continue to drive you crazy. He wants you to remain without the Spirit as long as possible so you won't have the power to defeat him. We don't need to tarry, though; we need simply to receive. Tell the devil that you're going to have a receiving service—not a tarrying service—to accept and possess God's gift!

I want what God has promised to me, don't you? I need power, joy, love, faith, and meekness, and I need them right now to do God's work. This is the very reason the devil doesn't want me to have them. He has confused this issue more than any other simply to keep men enslaved and to hinder God's work. If you have been bound by the devil's lies on this issue, it is time to shake free from his weak chains in the name of Jesus! It is time to repent, to get cleaned up in your spirit, and to receive God's gift of power and love. Now is the time to be baptized in the name of Jesus and receive the Holy Spirit. There's no need to tarry or wait.

Now, I'm not suggesting that God gives us everything we want simply for the asking. He doesn't work on a "name-it-claim-it" basis. What I am suggesting, though, is that we can be confident about receiving those things that God's Word has promised us. To those who believe on His name for salvation, He has already assured the gift of the Holy Spirit. As such, we can be confident that, in God's time, the Spirit's working will be evident in our lives.

# Receiving the Gift

"How do I receive His promised gift?" you ask. You receive it by humbly but boldly asking for it. You have to do the asking, the seeking, and the knocking. If your earthly father told you a wonderful new gift had been purchased for you—and that it was ready and waiting, all you had to do was ask—you would be confident in asking for it. You would say, "Dad, may I please have that gift?" In the same way, the gift of the Holy Spirit was made available to all Christians when Jesus died on the cross—but the asking must take place.

*Ask, and it shall be given you; seek, and ye shall find; knock, and it shall be opened unto you: for every one that asketh receiveth; and he that seeketh findeth; and to him that knocketh it shall be opened.*
(Matthew 7:7–8)

When you were out of the will of God, you spent more than enough time asking and seeking for the wrong things. Now is the time to ask for the good things of God, so you can do His work and live an overcomer's life. Happiness, strength, good health, prosperity, and power over the enemy can be found in Jesus. When you begin in faith to knock at the door of holiness, it will be opened unto you. When you ask the One who has all power to give you this gift of the Holy Spirit, He will answer your request.

*For every one that asketh receiveth; and he that seeketh findeth; and to him that knocketh it shall be opened. If a son shall ask bread of any of you that is a father, will he give him a stone? or if he ask a fish, will he for a fish give him a serpent? Or if he shall ask an egg, will he offer him a scorpion? If ye then, being evil, know how to give good gifts unto*

*your children: how much more shall your heavenly*
*Father give the Holy Spirit to them that ask him?*
(Luke 11:10–13)

In this passage, Jesus proved that "asking"—not "tarrying"—is the key to receiving the Holy Spirit. When you seek to find the door to God's New Testament promise of the Spirit, asking will unlock it. Once you're inside the door and the Giver has handed you the gift, it's your job to take it and move along in the power that has been given to you.

Perhaps one reason the disciples had to tarry in the book of Acts was because the Holy Spirit was making His debut. The promised baptism, or "clothing" of His power was promised by our resurrected Lord just before His ascension in Luke 24:49: *"Tarry ye in the city of Jerusalem, until ye be endued with power from on high."* He would come according to God's calendar, on the harvest festival Day of Pentecost as directed by God. But now that He has come, those who experience the Passover by accepting Jesus Christ, God's Passover Lamb, can receive the baptism of the Holy Spirit by simply asking in faith.

## No Cheerleading Needed!

The process is very simple indeed: We must only seek, knock, and ask; then the fullness of the Spirit will be given. But many people make it seem so difficult. Some teach that if you wait long enough, pray hard enough, scream loud enough, or say, "Thank You, Jesus—thank You, Jesus—thank You, Jesus," fast enough, you will receive the Holy Spirit. These techniques are equally unscriptural.

# Receiving the Gift

Scripture doesn't teach that Jesus' followers must get into prayer lines or create ritualistic pandemonium. The gift of the Spirit does not have to be conjured up or invoked as in some type of mystical séance. Those types of practices are man-made, and God isn't pleased with them. The Holy Spirit doesn't need a cheerleader to help Him out or to invoke His power; He can fill us with His presence without our help. All we need to do is repent and receive Jesus, be baptized in His name, and receive the Holy Spirit.

## The Key to Receiving: Hunger and Thirst

Desire is where it starts. Jesus said, *"Blessed are they which do hunger and thirst after righteousness: for they shall be filled"* (Matthew 5:6). There are two words you have to notice here: *"hunger"* and *"thirst."* These words imply a desire, a longing, a want, or a need. God gives to those who want what He has. He gives to those who do whatever it takes to receive the Holy Spirit. And this, in its simplest terms, is what constitutes faith.

> *But without faith it is impossible to please him: for he that cometh to God must believe that he is, and that he is a rewarder of them that diligently seek him.*
> (Hebrews 11:6)

Being hungry or thirsty implies that you need fulfillment, which causes you to come to God, believe that He is the Baptizer in the Holy Spirit, ask for the Holy Spirit, and receive the gift of His indwelling presence. Simple! God wants you to ask Him so that He can give. *"But my God shall supply all your need according to his riches in glory by Christ Jesus"* (Philippians 4:19).

God won't let your wants and needs go unattended, especially when your desire is to be more like Him. All you need to do is ask and receive, and He will bless your soul.

When I was filled with the Holy Spirit, not only was my newfound liberation in Christ less than acceptable through the eyes of my church, but I was considered to be in outright rebellion to the teaching set forth by the leaders. This was because of how I had received the Holy Spirit, which ultimately placed the authenticity of my gift on trial. In the end, my gift would be accepted by the congregation only if it was authenticated by man (blessed and certified by one of our elders) during a tarrying service at my church.

Needless to say, however, I had already been filled with the Holy Spirit days before in my bedroom at home. The Spirit of the Lord overwhelmed me, and as I began speaking in tongues, my mother, who was a Seventh-day Adventist, stood pounding on the other side of the door, demanding that I "Shut up all that noise!" So it wasn't through the laying on of hands or through a tarrying service that God ushered the Holy Spirit into my life; it was my faith, my desire, my hungering and thirsting that got His attention. That is why it's important for a person not just to know *about* Jesus, but to know Him in an intimate, personal way. It is only then that the Lord will develop in your life the real evidence of the Spirit, which is love.

If tarrying or the laying on of hands was your means for receiving the Holy Spirit, then you should not allow anyone, including me, to dispute the authenticity of your gift. Many have, in times past, received the Spirit's indwelling through both methods. But for others, such as myself, the method of simply asking and receiving is appropriate. It should neither be disputed nor belittled; instead it should be looked upon as a method that is in accordance with the Word of God.

## God Keeps His Promises

*Then Peter said unto them, Repent, and be baptized every one of you in the name of Jesus Christ for the remission of sins, and ye shall receive the gift of the Holy Ghost. For the promise is unto you, and to your children, and to all that are afar off, even as many as the Lord our God shall call.* (Acts 2:38–39)

The gift of the Holy Spirit is not a conjured-up religious façade but a promised gift from the Father to His children. If your natural father knocked on your door holding the keys to a brand new car, would you shun him and reject the gift? Would you tell him, "No, thank you. I'm satisfied just walking around. I don't need a car right now"? Of course not! Instead, you'd receive the gift with gladness. Likewise, we should exercise that same enthusiasm in receiving the greatest gift of all from the greatest Father of all—the gift of the Holy Spirit. Why walk when you can ride on His cloud of glory as He leads you on the best path for reaching your divine destiny?

The strategy of Lucifer, however, is to make you believe that receiving the gift of the Holy Spirit is of little or no significance. He would also have you believe that you must go through a long, drawn-out ritual. But the truth is, receiving the Holy Spirit *is* a very significant part of the Christian experience, and the only prerequisite for receiving the gift is salvation. One needs only to ask and have faith to receive.

# Empowered from Above

Regardless of how we receive the Holy Spirit, we must never lose focus on who is doing the actual filling. It's not by the hands of man that we are filled; it's by the hands of the heavenly Father as He places His Spirit, the divine Comforter and Guide, inside us.

Remember, the Spirit of God not only guides; He also changes us from the inside out. I often question those who claim to be filled but never change their character or the way they treat others. Such people never experience victory but remain in a constant state of depression and oppression. When you receive the precious gift of the Holy Spirit into your life, the Spirit in you is quickened any time you're tempted to engage in ungodly acts or behaviors. He supplies you with the fruit of the Spirit and the ability to draw strength from the Father in those times of weakness. No, the Holy Spirit is not a guarantee that life will be free of problems and temptations or that there will never be times of weakness. But with the Holy Spirit there will come guidance, warnings of oncoming danger, and peace in the midst of trials.

> *But the fruit of the Spirit is love, joy, peace, longsuffering, gentleness, goodness, faith, meekness, temperance: against such there is no law. And they that are Christ's have crucified the flesh with the affections and lusts. If we live in the Spirit, let us also walk in the Spirit. Let us not be desirous of vain glory, provoking one another, envying one another.*
>
> (Galatians 5:22–26)

Ask the One who has all power to fill you with His Spirit. Then His love, joy, and freedom will replace hate, depression, and oppression; His peace will remove anxiety;

# Receiving the Gift

His gentleness and goodness will overcome envy and strife; and His presence will turn disbelief into strong faith. Ask Him now so that you may come to experience the knowledge of His infinite wisdom and power.

# Chapter Five

## It All Comes Down to Love and Order

*M*y seventh dream came twenty days after the first night of dreams. I remember thinking, "Oh, Lord, I'm dreaming again." I knew something was happening, but I wasn't sure what. I didn't know if it was a dream or if it was a vision. I saw an enormous cloud being released. Then the messenger of the Lord said to me, "We must go to Calvary." And so we went back to Calvary. Once again I heard the unbearably loud screaming, the yelling, and the ringing of the hammer. Amid the noise and confusion, voices shouted out, "Give us Barabbas! Give us Barabbas!" I heard roosters crowing and voices crying, "I don't know Him! I don't know Him!" There were many voices.

*T*hen came the calm. The night changed to day as sunrise came. And there was violin music along with somber singing. I saw two women at the sepulchre; both were weeping and crying. And a messenger of the Lord said, "He is risen!"

*T*his was love.

# Chapter Five

# It All Comes Down to Love and Order

To understand the real evidence of God's Holy Spirit, we must refer once more to Paul's first letter to the Corinthians:

*Though I speak with the tongues of men and of angels, and have not charity, I am become as sounding brass, or a tinkling cymbal. And though I have the gift of prophecy, and understand all mysteries, and all knowledge; and though I have all faith, so that I could remove mountains, and have not charity, I am nothing.* (1 Corinthians 13:1–2)

Here Paul clearly named the fruit, or evidence, of the Spirit: love. Wouldn't you know it; right in the middle of this passage on spiritual gifts—including tongues—Scripture reminds us that love, not spiritual gifts, is the touchstone of the Spirit's indwelling! The Bible says that a tree is known by the fruit it bears. And the fruit, or evidence, of the Spirit is love. *"But the fruit of the Spirit is love, joy, peace, longsuffering, gentleness, goodness, faith, meekness, temperance: against such there is no law"* (Galatians 5:22–23).

Now if the gift of tongues was a fruit of the Spirit or evidence of His presence, it would have been listed here with the other fruits in Paul's definitive list. But it wasn't; instead, it was listed elsewhere in Scripture among the gifts of the Spirit.

Even though the Bible emphasizes tongues, it puts so much more emphasis on love. Paul's first letter to the Corinthians straightforwardly reminds us that everything, even the Spirit's gifts, are meaningless without love.

> *Though I speak with the tongues of men and of angels, and have not charity, I am become as sounding brass, or a tinkling cymbal. And though I have the gift of prophecy, and understand all mysteries, and all knowledge; and though I have all faith, so that I could remove mountains, and have not charity, I am nothing.* (1 Corinthians 13:1–2)

Notice that Paul named both of the Holy Spirit's speaking gifts—tongues and prophecy—along with knowledge and faith in this passage. He said you can have and use all those gifts—but if you don't have love, it doesn't profit you one bit!

So the *fruit* of the Spirit in our lives, not tongues, is the evidence that we are Christ's. Yet too many in our churches have focused on the gifts of the Spirit instead of His fruit. The apostle John wrote,

# It All Comes Down to Love and Order

*We know that we have passed from death unto life, because we love the brethren. He that loveth not his brother abideth in death.* (1 John 3:14)

In other words, you can speak in tongues all you want; if you don't love, though, you still abide in death. If you harbor hate in your heart, it doesn't matter how much you speak in tongues. *"Whosoever hateth his brother is a murderer: and ye know that no murderer hath eternal life abiding in him"* (v. 15). Love is the evidence of the Spirit.

## Is the Evidence Present in Your Life?

Examine your own life. Is the evidence of the Spirit present? Consider John's first epistle and the evidence of being filled with the Spirit that he described there:

*Beloved, let us love one another: for love is of God; and every one that loveth is born of God, and knoweth God. He that loveth not knoweth not God; for God is love.* (1 John 4:7–8)

*No man hath seen God at any time. If we love one another, God dwelleth in us, and his love is perfected in us. Hereby know we that we dwell in him, and he in us, because he hath given us of his Spirit.* (vv. 12–13)

*If a man say, I love God, and hateth his brother, he is a liar: for he that loveth not his brother whom he hath seen, how can he love God whom he hath not seen? And this commandment have we from him, That he who loveth God love his brother also.* (vv. 20–21)

87

Just as Paul emphasized the importance of love in his letters, so did John. John's works as a leader in the early church, as well as the works of the other apostles, were done in love. When they received the Holy Spirit, they received the love of God. This in turn led them to think of others' needs before their own. They were empowered with the Holy Spirit's love to fulfill Christ's teaching recorded in Matthew 25:35–36:

*For I was an hungered, and ye gave me meat: I was thirsty, and ye gave me drink: I was a stranger, and ye took me in: naked, and ye clothed me: I was sick, and ye visited me: I was in prison, and ye came unto me.*

If you have accepted Christ's gift of salvation, then this love is in your heart as well:

*And hope maketh not ashamed; because the love of God is shed abroad in our hearts by the Holy Ghost which is given unto us.* (Romans 5:5)

Sometimes love will lead you to sacrifice so that someone else can be helped. When you give to others without complaining or telling everyone that you gave, this is the love of God working in your life. And love extends beyond just our family and friends. When you are compassionate toward someone else's grandparents and visit them in the hospital, the love of God is working in your life. When it's not just your child in prison but someone else's whom you visit, this is the love of God working in your life. If you are a preacher and you go anywhere to preach the Gospel for free, whether your own congregation is there or not, this is the love of God working in your life. And when you do all these things in secret, when

# It All Comes Down to Love and Order

you don't broadcast them but keep them between God and yourself, this is good; this is God's love.

> *Charity suffereth long, and is kind; charity envieth not; charity vaunteth not itself, is not puffed up, doth not behave itself unseemly, seeketh not her own, is not easily provoked, thinketh no evil; rejoiceth not in iniquity, but rejoiceth in the truth; beareth all things, believeth all things, hopeth all things, endureth all things.* (1 Corinthians 13:4–7)

When you have the love of God, you can visibly see these characteristics of the Holy Spirit manifest in your life. Is such evidence present in your life? Do you love unconditionally? Do you show your love? Do you speak love to your brothers and sisters? We often say we love others, but do we really? Are we showing the fruit?

> *My little children, let us not love in word, neither in tongue; but in deed and in truth.* (1 John 3:18)

## Decently and In Order

> *Let all things be done decently and in order.* (1 Corinthians 14:40)

Closely related to love is the issue of order. We've already talked about how spiritual gifts, even the gift of tongues, mean nothing if the Spirit's fruit, or evidence, is absent. Similarly, spiritual gifts are no good unless we use them in the orderly fashion God has commanded. To use God's spiritual gifts in a disorderly way is both unloving toward our Christian brothers and sisters and disobedient toward God.

# Empowered from Above

Let's turn again to Paul's first letter to the Corinthians for guidance on the use of tongues:

> *Now, brethren, if I come unto you speaking with tongues, what shall I profit you, except I shall speak to you either by revelation, or by knowledge, or by prophesying, or by doctrine? And even things without life giving sound, whether pipe or harp, except they give a distinction in the sounds, how shall it be known what is piped or harped? For if the trumpet give an uncertain sound, who shall prepare himself to the battle? So likewise ye, except ye utter by the tongue words easy to be understood, how shall it be known what is spoken? for ye shall speak into the air. There are, it may be, so many kinds of voices in the world, and none of them is without signification. Therefore if I know not the meaning of the voice, I shall be unto him that speaketh a barbarian, and he that speaketh shall be a barbarian unto me....I thank my God, I speak with tongues more than ye all: yet in the church I had rather speak five words with my understanding, that by my voice I might teach others also, than ten thousand words in an unknown tongue.*
>
> (1 Corinthians 14:6–11, 18–19)

Here Paul addressed the "fleshly" problems the Corinthians were experiencing when they spoke in tongues. Notice that the same problem is present in many churches today. A lot of things are being done in the flesh instead of in the Spirit. Specifically, Paul said here that it doesn't make sense to get up in church and speak an unknown tongue to a congregation that can't understand a single word of it. This

# It All Comes Down to Love and Order

is an unloving and ungodly thing to do. It is more beneficial to edify and to help others than yourself. And when you speak in an unknown tongue, without an interpreter, others are not edified.

I believe that many in today's modern church have turned tongues into a "fad." They mistakenly believe it's popular to speak in an unknown tongue, even though the Holy Spirit may have nothing to do with it. These fad-seekers tend to think that speaking in tongues during church services will make them super-saints. This, however, is not scriptural. In fact, this mistaken belief was so widespread in Corinth that Paul devoted an entire chapter of 1 Corinthians to addressing it!

Don't get me wrong; Paul encouraged everyone to seek after the Spirit and receive the gift of tongues when it was given. But he also rebuked the church for its disorderly behavior and instructed its members to move only in God's spiritual order.

> *If therefore the whole church be come together into one place, and all speak with tongues, and there come in those that are unlearned, or unbelievers, will they not say that ye are mad? But if all prophesy, and there come in one that believeth not, or one unlearned, he is convinced of all, he is judged of all: and thus are the secrets of his heart made manifest; and so falling down on his face he will worship God, and report that God is in you of a truth.*
> (1 Corinthians 14:23–25)

In other words, Paul directed the Corinthian church to abstain from speaking in public tongues because of the confusion it could cause in the congregation. He did not condemn the use of public tongues; rather he instructed the Corinthian church on the importance of order, including the need for interpretation within a congregational use of tongues.

> *How is it then, brethren? when ye come together, every one of you hath a psalm, hath a doctrine, hath a tongue, hath a revelation, hath an interpretation. Let all things be done unto edifying. If any man speak in an unknown tongue, let it be by two, or at the most by three, and that by course; and let one interpret. But if there be no interpreter, let him keep silence in the church; and let him speak to himself, and to God. Let the prophets speak two or three, and let the other judge. If any thing be revealed to another that sitteth by, let the first hold his peace. For ye may all prophesy one by one, that all may learn, and all may be comforted. And the spirits of the prophets are subject to the prophets. For God is not the author of confusion, but of peace, as in all churches of the saints.*
> (1 Corinthians 14:26–33)

Paul, in essence, said, "Why is everyone flaunting his own abilities rather than edifying others and compelling them to Christ through the power of God? Someone needs edifying; someone needs help. And he can't get it because a group of people are living in the flesh and acting in ways that are totally out of order!"

Notice that Paul didn't say, "Let twenty speak and five interpret." No, he said, *"If any man speak in an unknown tongue, let it be by two, or at the most by three, and that by course; and let one interpret."* He also added, *"But if there be*

# It All Comes Down to Love and Order

*no interpreter, let him keep silence in the church; and let him speak to himself, and to God."*

"But pastor, I can't control it," someone says. That doesn't matter; the Lord isn't going to contradict His Word.

I have often spoken to people who say to me, "I just can't help myself! I speak in tongues at my job, in the grocery store, and I never know when the Spirit is going to provoke me to start speaking. And when I start, sometimes I just can't stop."

Well, I beg to differ with the "I just can't help myself" philosophy. Satan's practice is always to take what God meant for a blessing and turn it into a curse. As a believer, you should always live as one who *compels* others to come to Christ— not as one who *repels* them. Let us not ignore the instructions given in God's Word:

> *If therefore the whole church be come together into one place, and all speak with tongues, and there come in those that are unlearned, or unbelievers, will they not say that ye are mad? But if all prophesy, and there come in one that believeth not, or one unlearned, he is convinced of all, he is judged of all: and thus are the secrets of his heart made manifest; and so falling down on his face he will worship God, and report that God is in you of a truth. How is it then, brethren? when ye come together, every one of you hath a psalm, hath a doctrine, hath a tongue, hath a revelation, hath an interpretation. Let all things be done unto edifying. If any man speak in an unknown tongue, let it be by two, or at the most by three, and that by course; and let one interpret. But if there be*

*no interpreter, let him keep silence in the church; and let him speak to himself, and to God. Let the prophets speak two or three, and let the other judge. If any thing be revealed to another that sitteth by, let the first hold his peace. For ye may all prophesy one by one, that all may learn, and all may be comforted. And the spirits of the prophets are subject to the prophets. For God is not the author of confusion, but of peace, as in all churches of the saints.*

(1 Corinthians 14:23–33)

God is not one to send confusion. He is a God of peace and order. Whenever we lose focus, that which God has gifted to us as a blessing can become to us an unfortunate curse. God kept His promise by sending His Comforter; we must respond by keeping His Word, as well, by practicing to do *"all things...decently and in order"* (v. 40).

Being filled with the Holy Spirit is not a time for us as believers to flaunt our stuff and show the world how "holy" we are. Instead, it's a time to understand that it's not by our might, nor by our power, but by the Spirit of the Lord that we are able to be used for His glory. (See Zechariah 4:6.)

I encourage everyone—pastors, Sunday school teachers, elders, husbands, wives, and children alike—to read this chapter very carefully before entering your sanctuary doors for another service. May the Holy Spirit convict you to keep His good order.

# Chapter Six

## The Spirit's Unifying Work

*T*hen, in the spirit realm, I saw everyone who was in the Upper Room. People were everywhere, filling the streets, and they were all speaking different languages. And everyone was reunited with his or her loved ones because there was an interpreter that wasn't there in times past. Peter stood up, saying, "For these are not drunken, as ye suppose, seeing it is but the third hour of the day" (Acts 2:15).

*T*hen I looked up, and the messenger of the Lord said, "Behold, now: Satan's kingdom." And as I looked at Satan's kingdom and the principalities, there was mass confusion. Before, when the people prayed in their native languages, the demons had been able to write down what they said. On the Day of Pentecost, though, the saints stopped speaking their native tongues; they started speaking other tongues of men, and the door was opened for them to speak in the tongues of angels. And when they started praying in unknown tongues, the fallen angels could not unravel their prayers.

# Chapter Six

# The Spirit's Unifying Work

We've already talked about how the Holy Spirit serves as our Comforter, our Guide, and our Source of selfless love. But did you know He's a unifier, a mender of broken relationships? The Old Testament story of Daniel is a good place to further our study.

## Daniel's Sticky Situations

During the reign of Judah's King Jehoiakim, King Nebuchadnezzar of Babylon besieged Jerusalem. (See Daniel 1:1.) In overthrowing the government, he took the Israelites into captivity and carried them into the borders of Babylon. The king separated from the group those young men who were intelligent, wise, and without blemish, those considered most valuable and worthy of standing in the king's palace. (See Daniel 1:3–4.) Included in this group were Shadrach, Meshach, Abednego, and Daniel.

Even though Daniel found himself in captivity, he really was as free as can be. You see, when the Holy Spirit becomes your Guide, when you allow the Lord to direct your paths, captivity is only as bad as you allow it to be.

Maybe your bondage isn't physical, as Daniel's was. Maybe you're not behind bars or stuck in physical confinement but trapped instead by an oppressed mind, weaknesses, and failures. Nonetheless, you *can* maintain the victory that the Lord has given and draw from Him the strength that you need for difficult times. God's Word promises,

> *My grace is sufficient for thee: for my strength is made perfect in weakness. Most gladly therefore will I rather glory in my infirmities, that the power of Christ may rest upon me.* (2 Corinthians 12:9)

The Comforter is our gift from God. *"Not by might, nor by power, but by my spirit, saith the LORD of hosts"* (Zechariah 4:6).

Further in the book of Daniel we find that this man of God rose to a place of prominence, becoming ruler over the province of Babylon. What a leap for someone who was supposed to be a prisoner! But while the king respected Daniel's opinion, credibility, and devotion, others resented his favor with the king and conspired to ruin Daniel's credibility. When they found Daniel blameless, they conspired to attack the one thing that Daniel held most dear—his relationship with his God. (See Daniel 6:1–8.)

An application in this story for today is this: When the enemy finds you blameless, his next attempt is to hinder your communication with God. The devil knows that the Spirit of the Lord gives us knowledge and truth during prayer, which serves as a catalyst for our deliverance and victory; Satan wants to prevent us from receiving God's truth and knowledge. That's why he tries to impede our communication with God, just as he did with Daniel:

> *Then these presidents and princes assembled together to the king, and said thus unto him, King Darius, live for ever. All the presidents of the kingdom, the governors, and the princes, the counsellors, and the captains, have consulted together to establish a royal statute, and to make a firm decree, that whosoever shall ask a petition of any God or man for thirty days, save of thee, O king, he shall be cast into the den of lions.* (Daniel 6:6–7)

Because Daniel had the boldness of the Holy Ghost on his side and a solid relationship with the Lord, he was not deterred by this obvious attack. Instead he continued to pray as usual, three times a day with the windows open. Daniel was not afraid, nor would he submit to worshipping or praying to anything or anyone other than the true and living God. (See verse 10.) When the Holy Spirit is present, people do not shy away from issues; instead, they confront their situations with boldness and stand firm in what they believe.

Once he was found praying, Daniel was thrown into the den of lions. Because of the favor of the Lord upon Daniel's life, however, Daniel prevailed and the mouths of the lions were shut (Daniel 6:22). Daniel, because of his prayer life, was in direct contact with the Father and was accustomed to the Lord's answering His prayers. The Holy Spirit is indeed a Comforter; so even when our flesh resists and becomes anxious, we can count on Him to see us through every trial. Even when we are overwhelmed by life's situations and don't know how we should pray, the Holy Spirit intercedes for us. God's Word encourages us with this truth:

> *Likewise the Spirit also helpeth our infirmities: for we know not what we should pray for as we ought: but the Spirit itself maketh intercession for us with groanings which cannot be uttered.* (Romans 8:26)

The Greek word for *groan* simply means "articulation." The Spirit articulates our needs to the Father.

The Spirit doesn't speak Spanish, Greek, Chinese, or German, though; He speaks the language of heaven, a completely different language that allows our spirits to unite with His Spirit. Then He can intercede to God on our behalf. *"For if I pray in an unknown tongue, my spirit prayeth, but my understanding is unfruitful"* (1 Corinthians 14:14). You many not understand all that you're saying while speaking in tongues, but you know that God understands and He knows exactly what you need.

## An Awakening Dream: Insight into Daniel 10

I had never paid much attention to Daniel 10 until my seven-day dream, which specifically dealt with this Scripture passage and its meaning. In the dream I saw the entire world praying. I knew it was the entire world because I could see both night and day at once, and everyone was praying. As they were praying in cars, convalescent homes, open fields, shopping malls, and houses, a mist came out of their mouths; it floated up through ceilings and through roofs.

Then, as if suddenly snatched from this scene, I found myself traveling through the principalities of Satan. I never saw Lucifer himself, but I did see a man sitting on a throne with his hands resting over the arms of the chair. He had the most beautifully manicured nails. He was dressed in a white suit and had silky gray hair, which was neatly slicked back above his brow. I knew this man was Lucifer, even though His appearance was completely contrary to every image I'd ever had of Him. And that is one of the reasons the enemy of our souls is such a great deceiver; he doesn't wear a red suit, carry a pitchfork, or have horns and a long tail. He takes on a form that entices and draws others to him so that he can capture them in his web of deceit.

In my dream a great wall extended around the entire world. It was as if Satan had enclosed the whole world within a hedge. In every nook and cranny of the wall stood demons. As they looked at the wall, with pen and pads in hand, they recorded the prayers of the saints. Suddenly, I woke up, but the dream was still very vivid and lingered in my mind.

I later fell asleep again, only to return to the same dream. As the saints prayed, their prayers were plastered against the wall. The demons, which were disfigured animal-like creatures, wrote down the prayers of the saints. Suddenly I saw an angel come down out of the principalities. As the angel appeared, all the demons simultaneously wrestled him to the floor and pulled out of his hand what he had been holding. In the dream my body shook because God was showing me the reason that many of us don't get what God promises: We give up too easily. Every prayer that you pray is heard in Satan's kingdom, unless it is prayed in tongues. After the demons had wrestled the angel to the floor, I woke up. The Lord took me to Daniel 10.

*When I heard the voice of his words, then was I in a deep sleep on my face, and my face toward the ground. And, behold, an hand touched me, which set me upon my knees and upon the palms of my hands. And he said unto me, O Daniel, a man greatly beloved, understand the words that I speak unto thee, and stand upright: for unto thee am I now sent. And when he had spoken this word unto me, I stood trembling. Then said he unto me, Fear not, Daniel: for from the first day that thou didst set thine heart to understand, and to chasten thyself before thy God, thy words were heard, and I am come for thy words. But the prince of the kingdom of Persia withstood me one and twenty days: but, lo, Michael, one of the chief princes, came to help me; and I remained there with the kings of Persia. Now I am come to make thee understand what shall befall thy people in the latter days: for yet the vision is for many days.*
(Daniel 10:9–14)

It's clear, then, and important for us to understand, that we are fighting against supernatural forces that we cannot see. Many times our ministries are hindered because we allow spirits to wrestle God's angel down and rip from his hand the thing that God desires for us to have.

Finally God said, "Enough is enough. Every time I try to get a word to my people, they can't get it because Satan, the power of the air, hinders them from receiving the gifts I have to give. I'm going to change some things."

So now, when the saints begin to pray, the walls in the principalities are covered with tongues that no one can understand. Satan and his demonic hosts try, to no avail, to decode what is going on and to intercept the petitions of God's people. What they discover, though, is that the prayers on the wall can't be deciphered since tongues were born out of the shedding of Jesus' blood.

The saints of old used to sing a song, *"Oh, the blood of Jesus! It will never lose its power!"* God does have all power and His Son's blood is covering your prayers. Every time Satan tries to reach you and snatch you away from God's covering, he's forced to flee; he simply cannot deal with the blood of Christ.

In this way, the Holy Spirit is a unifier, a mender of the communication between God and His children. The work that Jesus began—to bring us back into communion with the Father—the Holy Spirit continues; He intercedes for us, presenting our requests to God in groanings that speak to God more completely and perfectly than our human tongues ever could.

## A Divided People

This story of Daniel provides the background for another unifying work of the Spirit: the reuniting of God's people with each other. You see, the people of Israel were divided, separated, scattered, and shattered during Daniel's time.

*In the third year of the reign of Jehoiakim king of Judah came Nebuchadnezzar king of Babylon unto Jerusalem, and besieged it. And the Lord gave Jehoiakim king of Judah into his hand, with part of the vessels of the house of God: which he carried into the land of Shinar to the house of his god; and he*

*brought the vessels into the treasure house of his*
*god.* (Daniel 1:1–2)

Without going into a lengthy study of Daniel 1, we can note that it contains a brief historical account of how several of the tribes of Judah were dispersed throughout the existing nations of the earth. Psalm 137:1–4 captures the emotions of Israel at that time:

*By the rivers of Babylon, there we sat down, yea, we wept, when we remembered Zion. We hanged our harps upon the willows in the midst thereof. For there they that carried us away captive required of us a song; and they that wasted us required of us mirth, saying, Sing us one of the songs of Zion. How shall we sing the Lord's song in a strange land?*

## The Hope for Dry Bones

The good news is, God did not leave Israel a shattered and scattered nation. He promised to bring it together again, to unite its people once more. One of the earliest and most vivid prophecies of this reuniting work is found in Ezekiel. There, the Lord led Ezekiel to a graveyard filled with bones, and miraculously He brought the bones together to form a body. As God brought these dead and separated graveyard bones together into new living forms, so too did He promise to restore Israel back to life. Let's take a look at Ezekiel 37:

*The hand of the Lord was upon me, and carried me out in the spirit of the Lord, and set me down in the midst of the valley which was full of bones, and caused me to pass by them round about: and,*

*behold, there were very many in the open valley;
and, lo, they were very dry. And he said unto me,
Son of man, can these bones live? And I answered,
O Lord GOD, thou knowest. Again he said unto me,
Prophesy upon these bones, and say unto them, O
ye dry bones, hear the word of the LORD. Thus saith
the Lord GOD unto these bones; Behold, I will cause
breath to enter into you, and ye shall live: and I will
lay sinews upon you, and will bring up flesh upon
you, and cover you with skin, and put breath in you,
and ye shall live; and ye shall know that I am the
LORD. So I prophesied as I was commanded: and
as I prophesied, there was a noise, and behold a
shaking, and the bones came together, bone to his
bone. And when I beheld, lo, the sinews and the
flesh came up upon them, and the skin covered
them above: but there was no breath in them. Then
said he unto me, Prophesy unto the wind, prophesy, son of man, and say to the wind, Thus saith the
Lord GOD; Come from the four winds, O breath, and
breathe upon these slain, that they may live. So I
prophesied as he commanded me, and the breath
came into them, and they lived, and stood up upon
their feet, an exceeding great army. Then he said
unto me, Son of man, these bones are the whole
house of Israel: behold, they say, Our bones are
dried, and our hope is lost: we are cut off for our
parts. Therefore prophesy and say unto them, Thus
saith the Lord GOD; Behold, O my people, I will
open your graves, and cause you to come up out of
your graves, and bring you into the land of Israel.
And ye shall know that I am the LORD, when I have*

*opened your graves, O my people, and brought you*
*up out of your graves, and shall put my spirit in*
*you, and ye shall live, and I shall place you in your*
*own land: then shall ye know that I the Lord have*
*spoken it, and performed it, saith the Lord.*

(Ezekiel 37:1–14)

Ezekiel 37:1 deals with traveling or entering into the vision of God. The next verse refers to the gathering of information. And the following verse is a challenge: *"Son of man, can these bones live?"* Ezekiel answered, *"O Lord God, thou knowest."* In other words, he was saying, "I am submitting myself to Your will. Whatever You say, I will do." In Ezekiel 37:4, God told Ezekiel to prophesy, which means "to proclaim," "to pre-announce," or "to preach." Ezekiel was admonished by the Lord to prophesy unto these bones, to decree to them, *"Hear the word of the Lord."*

Ezekiel was then carried into the great valley, through the collection of bones. Remember, *"the valley"* refers to a graveyard, and the graveyard in this particular text represents the nations in which Israel's people were trapped. The people of Israel were trapped in these nations for hundreds of years. Ezekiel was prophesying to a nation that was *"cut off for* [its] *parts"* (v. 11). Eventually the people of Israel would end up in Medes, Persia, Mesopotamia, Cyrene, and other nations. Ezekiel, however, brought a word of hope from God. The people of Israel had lost their identity, their hope, their ability to worship. Ezekiel reminded them of their history and of the promising future that lay ahead: the complete reunification of God's people with Himself and with each other.

# The Spirit's Unifying Work

## The Fulfillment: Pentecost

The fulfillment of Ezekiel's symbolic prophecy happened many years later, on the Day of Pentecost:

> *And there were dwelling at Jerusalem Jews, devout men, out of every nation under heaven. Now when this was noised abroad, the multitude came together, and were confounded, because that every man heard them speak in his own language. And they were all amazed and marvelled, saying one to another, Behold, are not all these which speak Galilaeans? And how hear we every man in our own tongue, wherein we were born? Parthians, and Medes, and Elamites, and the dwellers in Mesopotamia, and in Judaea, and Cappadocia, in Pontus, and Asia, Phrygia, and Pamphylia, in Egypt, and in the parts of Libya about Cyrene, and strangers of Rome, Jews and proselytes, Cretes and Arabians, we do hear them speak in our tongues the wonderful works of God. And they were all amazed, and were in doubt, saying one to another, What meaneth this?*
> (Acts 2:5–12)

Notice especially verse five: *"And there were dwelling at Jerusalem Jews, devout men, out of every nation under heaven."* The statement *"out of every nation under heaven"* is easy to understand. America did not exist at that time, neither did many other nations, states, and provinces that exist today. When the Word of God says, *"every nation under heaven,"* it's talking about the existing nations at that particular time, at the time of Pentecost. A list of some of those nations are given in verses nine and ten:

*Parthians, and Medes, and Elamites, and the dwellers
in Mesopotamia, and in Judaea, and Cappadocia, in
Pontus, and Asia, Phrygia, and Pamphylia, in Egypt,
and in the parts of Libya about Cyrene, and strangers
of Rome, Jews and proselytes, Cretes and Arabians.*

The Jewish people were living in all those nations.
The Jews who had been scattered during Daniel's time, the
Jews who had received Ezekiel's message of hope years
before—the ancestors of these scattered people now gathered together for the initial indwelling of the Holy Spirit. In
Acts 2 is the fulfillment of Ezekiel 38. The Holy Spirit once
more did a great unifying work.

## From Babel to Pentecost

The Tower of Babel can help us understand the unifying work of the Holy Spirit. Before we can gain this insight,
however, we need to review what happens when men try to
usurp God's authority.

*And the whole earth was of one language, and of
one speech. And it came to pass, as they journeyed
from the east, that they found a plain in the land
of Shinar; and they dwelt there. And they said one
to another, Go to, let us make brick, and burn them
thoroughly. And they had brick for stone, and slime
had they for mortar. And they said, Go to, let us build
us a city and a tower, whose top may reach unto
heaven; and let us make us a name, lest we be scattered abroad upon the face of the whole earth. And
the LORD came down to see the city and the tower,
which the children of men builded. And the LORD
said, Behold, the people is one, and they have all*

# The Spirit's Unifying Work

*one language; and this they begin to do: and now nothing will be restrained from them, which they have imagined to do. Go to, let us go down, and there confound their language, that they may not understand one another's speech. So the LORD scattered them abroad from thence upon the face of all the earth: and they left off to build the city. Therefore is the name of it called Babel; because the LORD did there confound the language of all the earth: and from thence did the LORD scatter them abroad upon the face of all the earth.* (Genesis 11:1–9)

At Babel, a king by the name of Nimrod was building a wonderful and glorious monument to himself, the type of monument that was built during ancient times. This reflected Nimrod's pride as well as the pride of the people; they thought they were going to build a tower up to the heavens. This really isn't too much different from the ambitions of many people today. The only difference between Nimrod's times and ours is that men no longer build the structured towers of Babel or ancient pyramids. We call them something different now: skyscrapers.

From the start of time, men have tried to reach the heavens relying only on human ingenuity. In our modern day, the race to reach the heavens thrives in corporate America. From the CNN Towers of Toronto, Canada, to the Empire State Building of New York City, and the Sears Tower of Chicago, Illinois, man, in his quest to reach the heavens for power, wisdom, and knowledge, has not detoured from ancient mystical beliefs that the sky can be reached. In corporate America, the floor you are on suggests the level of your success and power. A corner office on the top floor of a tall building with windows overlooking the city implies that you have really reached the heavens.

So this young man, Nimrod, was approached by his astrologers and chief priests to build a temple that would allow them to reach into the heavens. As they called in their architects and designers, the ideal architectural plan was finally completed. By one historian's account of archeological findings, the tower of Babel was built thousands of feet into the sky. One of the things you can't deny is that, during this time when there were no cranes or modern technology of any sort, these men completed quite a feat. They came to a place of oneness where almost anything was possible.

Much to the amazement of everyone, although this structure was already so high, they decided to build it a little higher. They also began constructing a dome, a place for the priests and astrologers to conduct their work by studying the heavens and the stars. And God became angry. God became angry because the inhabitants of the earth decided to try to enter heaven without coming through the doorway of righteousness. They used what they thought would be a mighty power force—they used unity. When a body is unified, it can do almost anything.

The Scriptures say that they were of one mind, one heart, and that they could do anything.

> *And the LORD said, Behold, the people is one, and they have all one language; and this they begin to do: and now nothing will be restrained from them, which they have imagined to do.* (Genesis 11:6)

# The Spirit's Unifying Work

It is here that God released a spirit of confusion, which is how the tower got its name. In a split second, men began to speak other languages that sounded like babble to each other.

*Go to, let us go down, and there confound their language, that they may not understand one another's speech. So the LORD scattered them abroad from thence upon the face of all the earth: and they left off to build the city. Therefore is the name of it called Babel; because the LORD did there confound the language of all the earth: and from thence did the LORD scatter them abroad upon the face of all the earth.*
(Genesis 11:7–9)

After chattering from one person to the other, they began to find partners whom they could understand. The Scripture says that they began to form regencies and camps, then countries and nations.

Now one may ask, "What is the relationship between Babel and Pentecost?" The answer is simple. In Genesis 11, God used tongues to divide the nations. But in Acts 2, He used tongues to bring the nations back together. The hope that was lost at Babel was reclaimed at Pentecost. So Pentecost not only releases the church; it also brings into focus God's long-term plan to bring us back to our first love.

*And when the day of Pentecost was fully come, they were all with one accord in one place. And suddenly there came a sound from heaven as of a rushing mighty wind, and it filled all the house where they were sitting. And there appeared unto them cloven tongues like as of fire, and it sat upon each of them.*
(Acts 2:1–3)

# Chapter Seven

# From Death to Life— Raised to Serve

*It dawned on me that my dreams started on the commemorated Day of Pentecost, Pentecost Sunday. I realized that God was revealing to me the purpose of Pentecost—the purpose of 120 individuals in the Upper Room, the purpose of the outpouring of the Spirit. He was revealing to me how dirty vessels will be made clean and how, through His blood, He would take dirty water and turn it into wine.*

*Scripture became so alive to me in my dreams that the rumbling of a great cloud beneath me became the moaning and groaning, the travailing of God in the Spirit, as He gave birth to the Holy Ghost on earth. He was waiting, though, for the 120 vessels to come together in one accord, in the same mind for a moment, so they could house His presence. He could then make His entrance onto the earth and combat the demonic forces of the ages that were eagerly waiting to attack the earth.*

*T*hrough the propitiation and regeneration effected by the blood of the Lamb, the prophecy of a wedding at Cana had now come to pass on the Day of Pentecost. As recorded in the gospel of John, Jesus was invited to the wedding. When they ran out of wine, Jesus asked for six waterpots. These waterpots were nothing short of bathtubs where the people washed their feet after their long journeys on dusty roads. For the Scripture says, "There were set there six waterpots of stone, after the manner of the purifying of the Jews, containing two or three firkins [twenty to thirty gallons] apiece" (John 2:6). These pots were used for cleaning. And it was these—these dirty, dingy pots—that were brought to Jesus.

*A*nd He commanded them to be filled with water, representing life. Empty vessels were filled with water, life, the Spirit of God. The transforming power that took place at Pentecost was the same power Christ used when He turned water into wine. The Holy Spirit—pure, clean, and perfect—filled and transformed empty vessels, and He continues that work to this day.

# Chapter Seven

# From Death to Life—
# Raised to Serve

The breath of God's Spirit has always been the source of His life-producing plan. The Old Testament prophet Ezekiel learned this through God's amazing prophetic picture: Just as the lifeless skeletal bones formed a body, dead and defeated Israel would come to life.

> *Thus saith the Lord GOD unto these bones; Behold, I will cause breath to enter into you, and ye shall live: and I will lay sinews upon you, and will bring up flesh upon you, and cover you with skin, and put breath in you, and ye shall live; and ye shall know that I am the LORD. So I prophesied as I was commanded: and as I prophesied, there was a noise, and behold a shaking, and the bones came together, bone to his bone.* (Ezekiel 37:5–7)

# Empowered from Above

God's Spirit brought life again when Jesus breathed the breath of life back into the disciples, Adam's descendants. These were the first human beings to receive God's re-creative life as born-again men.

> *Then said Jesus to them again, Peace be unto you: as my Father hath sent me, even so send I you. And when he had said this, he breathed on them, and saith unto them, Receive ye the Holy Ghost.*
>
> (John 20:21–22)

God's breath brought new life at the Day of Pentecost too. The disciples who stayed in Jerusalem were visited by a mighty rushing wind.

> *And suddenly there came a sound from heaven as of a rushing mighty wind, and it filled all the house where they were sitting.* (Acts 2:2)

God always has a purpose in breathing new life into His children. Once He saves us and fills us, He wants to use us. Those who were faithful and stayed in Jerusalem for Pentecost were never the same again; as the book of Acts later tells us, they turned the world upside down. (See Acts 17:6.) God desires to do the same through each of His children. Let's prepare ourselves to receive His life-giving, life-restoring, life-changing breath.

## When We Hear God's Word, We Must Confess

> *If thou shalt confess with thy mouth the Lord Jesus, and shalt believe in thine heart that God hath raised him from the dead, thou shalt be saved.*
>
> (Romans 10:9)

# From Death to Life—Raised to Serve

As we've seen through scriptural accounts of God's life-giving Spirit, people without the energizing breath of the Holy Spirit are mere shadows of what they can be. God's life-changing anointing, though, falls only upon His truth. His anointing, His Spirit, His life, will not come to the one who is ignorant of His ways. If we hope to receive His life-giving breath, our lives must be steeped in Scripture, God's means for imparting truth. It is the Word that brings the truth and ultimately makes us free. (See John 8:32.) As Jesus said in John 6:63, *"It is the spirit that quickeneth; the flesh profiteth nothing: the words that I speak unto you, they are spirit, and they are life."* Every time we hear the Word of the Lord, our spirits are being quickened, or made alive.

Not only must we immerse our own minds and spirits in God's Word; we also need to share His truth with others around us!

> *And how shall they preach, except they be sent? as it is written, How beautiful are the feet of them that preach the gospel of peace, and bring glad tidings of good things!* (Romans 10:15)

As Ezekiel was commanded to, *"Prophesy upon these bones, and say unto them, O ye dry bones, hear the word of the LORD"* (Ezekiel 37:4), we too must proclaim the Word of the Lord. Remember, God set Ezekiel in the midst of a graveyard, in the midst of skeletons desperately in need of new life. And remember too that God provided Ezekiel with the words to say, with the message of hope that would bring life. As you obey God and listen for His leading in your life, He will set you among breathless bones craving life. And He will provide you with the wisdom to share His life-giving Word.

# Empowered from Above

## God Is Building an Army

*So I prophesied as he commanded me, and the breath came into them, and they lived, and stood up upon their feet, an exceeding great army.*

(Ezekiel 37:10)

Another thing Ezekiel showed us is that when the Word of God speaks, we must recognize our own potential. Just as God raised those dry bones and assembled them into a great army, God wants to clean us up and arm us for the great spiritual battle we're facing.

*Finally, my brethren, be strong in the Lord, and in the power of his might. Put on the whole armour of God, that ye may be able to stand against the wiles of the devil. For we wrestle not against flesh and blood, but against principalities, against powers, against the rulers of the darkness of this world, against spiritual wickedness in high places. Wherefore take unto you the whole armour of God, that ye may be able to withstand in the evil day, and having done all, to stand. Stand therefore, having your loins girt about with truth, and having on the breastplate of righteousness; and your feet shod with the preparation of the gospel of peace; above all, taking the shield of faith, wherewith ye shall be able to quench all the fiery darts of the wicked. And take the helmet of salvation, and the sword of the Spirit, which is the word of God.*

(Ephesians 6:10–17)

When you hear the truth about your own situation, the best thing you can do is accept it and be obedient to the

# From Death to Life—Raised to Serve

Lord's holy call, even if He leads you into a frightening situation, like facing the enemies' fiery darts. You must believe the Word of the Lord, which says, "[I] *shall put my spirit in you, and ye shall live*" (Ezekiel 37:14). For, *"I can do all things through Christ which strengtheneth me"* (Philippians 4:13).

When the Lord told His disciples that they would receive power after the Holy Ghost came upon them, this gave them hope that they would be able to accomplish what the Lord had called them to do.

*And, behold, I send the promise of my Father upon you: but tarry ye in the city of Jerusalem, until ye be endued with power from on high. And he led them out as far as to Bethany, and he lifted up his hands, and blessed them. And it came to pass, while he blessed them, he was parted from them, and carried up into heaven. And they worshipped him, and returned to Jerusalem with great joy: and were continually in the temple, praising and blessing God. Amen.* (Luke 24:49–53)

Before they heard of their potential, they didn't really know how they would be able to be witnesses for Christ. The promise of God's power, though, and His assurance of their potential in Him made the difference.

So once you hear and read in the Word of God about your potential, about your glorious destiny in life, it's time to stand up to be trained as a soldier. You can be as confident as the disciples in knowing He'll lead you to be everything He said you can be.

# Empowered from Above

*And I will lay sinews upon you, and will bring up flesh upon you, and cover you with skin, and put breath in you, and ye shall live; and ye shall know that I am the LORD.* (Ezekiel 37:6)

You can rest in knowing that God will restore you and lead you through life's stages. You must be willing, though, to grow through those stages. Hearing the Word of God will bring the Holy Spirit into your life. But merely hearing the Word makes no one complete. If we want to grow and mature to become all that we can be, an obedient response is necessary. *"For as the body without the spirit is dead, so faith without works is dead also"* (James 2:26). In order to become complete, we must first take steps in the Christian life.

*But we all, with open face beholding as in a glass the glory of the Lord, are changed into the same image from glory to glory, even as by the Spirit of the Lord.* (2 Corinthians 3:18)

The story of Ezekiel's prophecy provides an image of this step-by-step process. The first step in Ezekiel's prophecy showed breath assembling dead, dry bones. Next came the sinews. And then came the flesh. Hearing and obeying are both parts of a step-by-step, orderly process, just as the assembling of the bones was a step-by-step operation. There's more to the process of becoming a powerful soldier than being born again. If receiving God's gift was all it took to walk victoriously in this life, simply sitting in church or hanging around the barracks while others trained would be good enough. But it's not. James reminded us that if believing was all it took to walk in the fullness of God's life, even Satan's devils would be saved.

# From Death to Life—Raised to Serve

*Thou believest that there is one God; thou doest well: the devils also believe, and tremble. But wilt thou know, O vain man, that faith without works is dead?*
(James 2:19–20)

Faith, the obedient response to every word of God, is what takes us through God's step-by-step process for becoming soldiers in life. Romans 10:17 says, *"Faith cometh by hearing, and hearing by the word of God."* But it is the obedient response to every word of God that puts flesh on the bones of our Christian walk from glory to glory and faith to faith.

*For I am not ashamed of the gospel of Christ: for it is the power of God unto salvation to every one that believeth; to the Jew first, and also to the Greek. For therein is the righteousness of God revealed from faith to faith: as it is written, The just shall live by faith.*
(Romans 1:16–17)

## Broken Lives Method

Are you having a hard time picturing yourself as a soldier? Are you having difficulty hearing and accepting God's potential for your life?

Remember, Ezekiel 37:2 says the bones were dry and without life. God will move in lifeless situations. He is always ready to impart His Spirit to any who will confess the dryness and deadness of their lives. Just because you have a hard time picturing yourself as a life-filled fighting soldier in God's army doesn't mean it won't happen. Ezekiel's prophetic picture shows how the broken pieces of our lives come together in God's special mending once we accept and obey His sovereign Word.

# Empowered from Above

*So I prophesied as I was commanded: and as I prophesied, there was a noise, and behold a shaking, and the bones came together, bone to his bone.*
(Ezekiel 37:7)

God's mending process is not always easy. If we are to become God's powerful army, we first have to be shaken out of everything that is not of God. We need to be shaken out of our comfort zones of denominational doctrines and rulebooks; we need to be torn away from sin, witchcraft, evil doings, jealousy, and division. His Holy Spirit will do it once you respond to His Word. And when God begins to speak to you, He will mend your broken dreams. There will be a shaking as the pieces of your life come back together to form His image of you. As He brought Ezekiel's broken bones together to form a powerful army, He will gather the dead, dry pieces of your life and breathe His life-changing Spirit into them.

*Then said he unto me, Prophesy unto the wind, prophesy, son of man, and say to the wind, Thus saith the Lord GOD; Come from the four winds, O breath, and breathe upon these slain, that they may live.*
(v. 9)

Notice that the wind of God's Spirit in Ezekiel's vision came from the four winds, or the four corners of the earth. Ezekiel's prophetic vision encourages us to know that there isn't any area of our lives that God can't fill with His Holy Spirit. God's Word will speak truth into our spirits universally. Our broken pasts, our loneliness, our wounds, and our disappointments can all be healed—restored and made brand-new from the north, south, east, and west.

## From Death to Life—Raised to Serve

The Spirit of God will tell you to live. His truth will speak into your barrenness and cause your womb to open. He will tell you to be healed, encourage you when you're discouraged, speak hope when you're hopeless, and bring life out of death. The Comforter, Teacher, Helper, and Guide will come to whosoever calls upon Him. He will make them new creatures with born-again lives.

Focus on what you hear from God instead of the negatives that float around you every day. Know that the Holy Spirit will fill and renew the dry, dead areas of your life. Report every day for new instructions as a soldier in God's army. Open yourself to His gifts. Don't forbid the gift of tongues. Be available to receive His gift of prophecy and other spiritual gifts. Be sensitive when God may be sending someone to you with an encouraging word. Look for His truth daily in the pages of Scripture. And, above all, stay in order. As you grow from faith to faith, He will use you to breathe new life into others. He will keep you fresh within the powerful, peaceful flow of His mighty rushing wind. And God will receive the glory as He completes His work through us.

# Afterword

## The Benefits of Baptism

# Afterword

# The Benefits of Baptism

In a familiar old hymn, the songwriter asked, "What can wash away my sins?" and then responded, "Nothing but the blood of Jesus." We make a huge mistake when we allow ourselves to believe that the water itself will wash away our sins. Let us examine Acts 2:37–38:

> *Now when they heard this, they were pricked in their heart, and said unto Peter and to the rest of the apostles, Men and brethren, what shall we do? Then Peter said unto them, Repent, and be baptized every one of you in the name of Jesus Christ for the remission of sins, and ye shall receive the gift of the Holy Ghost.*

When Peter instructed his listeners to *"be baptized...for the remission of sins,"* he was not saying that they had to be baptized in order to have their sins forgiven. On the contrary, their sins were forgiven once they repented and received Jesus Christ as Lord and Savior; baptism was then an outward sign of the inward work in these listeners' lives. The same is true today; confessing Jesus as Lord is the only route to salvation. The Bible is very clear on this:

*That if thou shalt confess with thy mouth the Lord Jesus, and shalt believe in thine heart that God hath raised him from the dead, thou shalt be saved.*
(Romans 10:9)

*I am the way, the truth, and the life: no man cometh unto the Father, but by me.* (John 14:6)

The sprinkling of water or the submersion into water, then, is not a tool for salvation. Instead, the water becomes a symbolic grave: The person being baptized represents the body, submersion into water represents the burial of that body, and rising out of the water represents resurrection— dying to this world and rising to walk in the newness of life.

## The Baptism of the Beloved Son

When Jesus was baptized by John the Baptist, the emphasis was not on the water; it was on the Holy Spirit. John said,

*I indeed baptize you with water unto repentance: but he that cometh after me is mightier than I, whose shoes I am not worthy to bear: he shall baptize you with the Holy Ghost, and with fire.* (Matthew 3:11)

When Jesus rose out of the water, the heavens opened up. And once you die to sin, the heavens open up to you as well. When the heavens opened up at Christ's baptism, representing revelation from God, the voice of God spoke a heavenly proclamation of an earthly standing: *"This is my beloved*

# Afterword: The Benefits of Baptism

*Son, in whom I am well pleased"* (Matthew 3:17). Then the Spirit of God descended as a dove.

In Scripture, John introduced Jesus as the Lamb of God. *"The next day John seeth Jesus coming unto him, and saith, Behold the Lamb of God, which taketh away the sin of the world"* (John 1:29). And as Matthew 3:17 records, God introduced Jesus as His beloved Son. Jesus is the Lamb, who takes away the sins of the world. And He is the beloved Son of God, the only Doorway into the kingdom of heaven. *"I am the way, the truth, and the life: no man cometh unto the Father, but by me"* (John 14:6). Again, Jesus—not the act of baptism—is the only way to salvation.

Understanding baptism through study takes the chilly water of Jordan and turns it into a river of life, springing up from everlasting to everlasting. We need to understand, though, the difference between baptism in the Holy Spirit and being filled with the Holy Spirit; these are two separate experiences. Before our salvation, the Holy Spirit convicts us of sin and introduces us to Christ Jesus. The dispensational work of the filling of the Holy Spirit, however, begins at redemption.

Now, let's look at the life of Jesus. Jesus stepped into the water and was baptized of John's baptism. Immediately after he came out of the water, the heavens opened up. So the earthly baptism always triggers something in the heavenly realm. And on the Day of Pentecost, the earthly baptism of Christ triggered something in the heavenly realm.

*And when the day of Pentecost was fully come, they were all with one accord in one place. And suddenly there came a sound from heaven as of a rushing mighty wind, and it filled all the house where they were sitting. And there appeared unto them cloven tongues like as of fire, and it sat upon each of them. And they were all filled with the Holy Ghost, and began to speak with other tongues, as the Spirit gave them utterance.* (Acts 2:1–4)

Jesus was baptized physically by John. The heavens then opened up, and the Spirit of God descended like a dove. This means that the first work was done for repentance, as an outward sign of an inward work; the Holy Spirit descending as a dove, though, was God's sending a manifestation of His power. The coming of the Holy Spirit symbolized that Jesus was not only baptized on the earth but was also baptized from above.

After His baptism, Jesus was led out of the water and into the wilderness where He fasted for forty days and forty nights. *"Then was Jesus led up of the Spirit into the wilderness to be tempted of the devil"* (Matthew 4:1). Notice that the devil didn't begin tempting Jesus until His season of fasting had ended. Understand that if you are going to be a prayer warrior, the devil is not going to attack you while you are going to prayer; he's going to attack you after you are finished praying because he wants to challenge what God has shown you, and he wants you to curse God.

After Jesus completed the fast, Satan came. *"And when he had fasted forty days and forty nights, he was afterward an hungered. And...the tempter came to him"* (vv. 2–3). As recorded in Matthew 4:3–10, the tempter came to tempt Jesus with many things. Jesus would not have been able to deal with those attacks had He not been baptized from above.

# Afterword: The Benefits of Baptism

## Why Should I Get Baptized?

Now after learning all this, you may ask the question, "What am I going to receive if I get baptized?" A few benefits of baptism are as follows. Baptism

- ✤ announces to the world your changed life
- ✤ gives you access to divine revelation
- ✤ endows you with power from on high
- ✤ gives you the right to use the name of Jesus
- ✤ establishes you in the principalities
- ✤ secures your home in glory after departing this life

Baptism allows you to leave dead issues and ungodly spirits down in the water, freeing you to hear the voice of God with clarity and understanding. It is your confession of Christ that allows these sins to stay buried, never to be resurrected again. Whenever you feel these issues or ungodly spirits trying to creep back into your life, you need simply to speak the Word! Confess that your baptism was more than a chilly experience, that now you're walking in newness of life.

When you receive baptism into your life, you are going to begin receiving divine revelation. And this divine revelation will reveal to you truths that God could not tell you before you went into the water. Baptism brings you into the body of Christ, connecting you with other believers. It is through baptism that God knits His children together into a unified body.

Before I really understood baptism, I was baptized four or five times. Once I got it right, though, I realized that there were some things God wanted to tell me and show me that He couldn't reveal to me beforehand. Understand that baptism is not a ritual but is indeed a spiritual experience with God. Although you may still have issues that you need to deal with after baptism, you will soon see the doorway of revelation that God has been trying to show you. Baptism will unlock every prison door in your life. Baptism connects you with God. Don't underestimate its many benefits.

# Life Application

---

# Study Guide

# &

# Personal Journal

Chapter One

# The Purpose of Pentecost

*Read Acts 2:1–21. Those in the Upper Room had to wait on God for days with full unity of purpose before they received the Holy Spirit, a task that most Christians today would have a hard time completing. Are you waiting on God every day? Are your times with other Christians marked by unity or by dissension?*

# Life Application: Study Guide & Personal Journal

*What specifically about the indwelling of the Holy Spirit and the gifts of prophecy and tongues has confused you in the past? How has that confusion been dispelled through your reading of this first chapter? As you continue to read, examine your own thoughts concerning the gifts of the Spirit and consciously search to be sure they are in accord with what Scripture says.*

Chapter Two

# Who Is This Holy Spirit?

*Several words and phrases are used throughout this chapter to describe the Spirit. List some of them below and explain how you have experienced those characteristics of the Spirit in your own life.*

_____

_____

_____

_____

_____

_____

_____

_____

_____

_____

_____

_____

_____

_____

_____

_____

_____

_____

_____

_____

*Read Matthew 26:39. Jesus hoped for God's will to be done in another way besides His death on the cross, but He submitted Himself to God's purpose. Jesus knew He was placed on earth to follow God's will, even to the Cross.*

*Are you showing this same submission? Or have you acted as if the Holy Spirit exists to do your bidding? How can you make sure that it is God's will you are pursuing and not your own?*

Chapter Three

# Why Tongues?

*Read Acts 1:8. The universal evidence of baptism in the Spirit is power. Have you received this power? How are you using it?*

_____

_____

_____

_____

_____

_____

_____

_____

_____

_____

_____

_____

_____

_____

_____

_____

_____

_____

_____

# Life Application: Study Guide & Personal Journal

*According to Acts 1:8, the disciples were to use the Spirit's power to witness in Jerusalem and abroad. Are you witnessing and ministering to others? How can you use the power of the Holy Spirit to minister more effectively?*

Chapter Four

# Receiving the Gift

*First Corinthians 14:1 says we should "desire spiritual gifts." Are you holding back from receiving God's gifts for you? Are you "tarrying"? If so, why? What changes can you make in your life so that you are able to fully receive the Holy Spirit's gifts?*

_____

_____

_____

_____

_____

_____

_____

_____

_____

_____

_____

_____

_____

_____

_____

_____

_____

# Life Application: Study Guide & Personal Journal

*What are your spiritual gifts? Tell God that you desire to be filled with whatever gifts He wishes to bestow upon you. Pray also that your gifts would be made clear to you and that you would use them for His glory.*

_____

_____

_____

_____

_____

_____

_____

_____

_____

_____

_____

_____

_____

_____

_____

_____

_____

_____

_____

_____

_____

_____

_____

_____

Chapter Five

# It All Comes Down to Love and Order

*Read what 1 Corinthians 13:1–2 and Galatians 5:22–23 say about love, the fruit of the Spirit. How is love evidenced in your life? What are the characteristics of love that you should be displaying? How are you showing love to your family, coworkers, and fellow church members?*

# Life Application: Study Guide & Personal Journal

*Read 1 Corinthians 14:40. Are you using the gifts of the Spirit "decently and in order"? What motivates your actions during public worship? Are you trying to draw attention to yourself, or are you using the Spirit's gifts for the edification of your church in an orderly manner? Pray that your worship would reflect your God as a God of peace and order.*

Chapter Six

# The Spirit's Unifying Work

*Read Psalm 137:1–4. Do these words correspond to your own feelings of captivity? What specifically is holding you captive? With the Lord's help, identify what these prison bars are made of and prayerfully seek His freeing work. Pray that you too will learn to sing the Lord's song again.*

*Do the stories of the dry bones and the Tower of Babel remind you of division in your own family or church? How? Express your thankfulness to God for His Spirit's unifying work, and pray that God would use you to bring unity to these areas of division.*

_____

_____

_____

_____

_____

_____

_____

_____

_____

_____

_____

_____

_____

_____

_____

_____

_____

Chapter Seven

# From Death to Life—Raised to Serve

*Read Genesis 2:7 and Ezekiel 37:6. We are called to be soldiers for Christ. How can your dry bones be restored so that you are able to join God's army with flesh and sinew intact? What steps must you take to receive God's life-giving breath?*

_____

_____

_____

_____

_____

_____

_____

_____

_____

_____

_____

_____

_____

_____

_____

_____

_____

_____

# Life Application: Study Guide & Personal Journal

*Read Ephesians 6:10–17. What spiritual battle are you facing today? How can you train and equip yourself so that you are able to fight well? How should you dress yourself spiritually? What should you do if you begin to feel fear or doubt as to the outcome of the battle?*

_____

_____

_____

_____

_____

_____

_____

_____

_____

_____

_____

_____

_____

_____

_____

_____

_____

_____

_____

_____

# About the Author

# About the Author

# George Bloomer

Bishop George G. Bloomer is a native of Brooklyn, New York. After serving as an evangelist for fourteen years, Dr. Bloomer began pastoring in 1996. He is the founder and senior pastor of Bethel Family Worship Center in Durham, North Carolina, but continues to travel extensively, sharing with others his testimony of how the Lord delivered him from a life of poverty, drug abuse, sexual abuse, and mental anguish. "God had a plan for my life," Bloomer now says, "and even during my span of lawlessness, the angels of the Lord were protecting me because the call of God was upon my life."

Bloomer holds the degree of Doctor of Religious Arts in Christian Psychology and conducts many seminars dealing with relationships, finances, and stress management. He is founder of Young Witnesses for Christ, a youth evangelistic outreach ministry with several chapters on college campuses throughout the United States, and bishop of C.L.U.R.T (Come Let Us Reason Together) International Assemblies, comprised of over 80 churches nationwide and abroad. His message is one of deliverance and of a hope that far exceeds the desperation and oppression of many silent sufferers.

# ANOTHER POWERFUL BOOK
## from Whitaker House

**Crazy House, Sane House**
*George and Jeannie Bloomer*

Too many couples have spent years building their relationship
on shifting, unstable foundations, just to see it all come to a
tragic end. George and Jeannie Bloomer lead you through the
various phases of constructing a strong and peaceful home,
showing you how to prevent or repair the structural damage
that can bring pain to a relationship. Discover the keys to
building a strong house, a strong marriage, and a strong future.

ISBN: 0-88368-726-7 • Trade • 144 pages

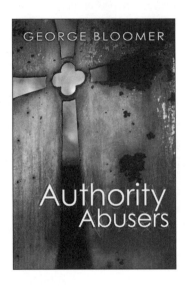

# OTHER POWERFUL BOOKS
## from Whitaker House

### Understanding the Purpose and Power of Woman
Dr. Myles Munroe

To live successfully in the world, women need to know who they are and what role they play today. They need a new awareness of who they are, and new skills to meet today's challenges. Myles Munroe helps women to discover who they are. Whether you are a woman or a man, married or single, this book will help you to understand the woman as she was meant to be.

ISBN: 0-88368-671-6 • Trade • 208 pages

### Understanding the Purpose and Power of Men
Dr. Myles Munroe

Today, the world is sending out conflicting signals about what it means to be a man. Many men are questioning who they are and what roles they fulfill in life—as a male, a husband, and a father. Best-selling author Myles Munroe examines cultural attitudes toward men and discusses the purpose God has given them. Discover the destiny and potential of the man as he was meant to be.

ISBN: 0-88368-725-9 • Trade • 224 pages

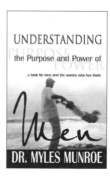

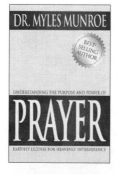

### Understanding the Purpose and Power of Prayer
Dr. Myles Munroe

All that God is—and all that God has—may be received through prayer. Everything you need to fulfill your purpose on earth is available to you through prayer. The biblically-based, time-tested principles presented here will ignite and transform the way you pray. Be prepared to enter into a new dimension of faith, a deeper revelation of God's love, and a renewed understanding that your prayers can truly move the finger of God.

ISBN: 0-88368-442-X • Trade • 240 pages

# OTHER POWERFUL *B*OOKS

## from Whitaker House

### The Secret Place
*Dr. Dale A. Fife*

You hunger to live in the presence of God. You yearn to know the Father's heart in an intimate way. You desire revelation and passionate encounters with the Almighty. You long to spend time in the Secret Place, getting to know the Father in a deeper way. If you long to experience a greater intimacy with the Father, *The Secret Place* will draw you in and change your life!

ISBN: 0-88368-715-1 • Trade • 240 pages

### The Anatomy of God
*Dr. Kenneth Ulmer*

Throughout Scripture, God describes Himself in anatomical terms we are familiar with. His eyes wink and squint. His mouth whispers, His smile radiates, and He inclines an ear to our cries. In *The Anatomy of God,* Dr. Kenneth Ulmer introduces us to a God who is touchable, emotional, and accessible. If you desire to know God in a deeper way, or even if you question His closeness and concern, allow *The Anatomy of God* to draw you closer to Him.

ISBN: 0-88368-711-9 • Trade • 208 pages